A YEAR IN WICKLOW WITH MICKO

COMHAIRLE CHONTAE ÁTHA CLIATH THEAS
SOUTH DUBLIN COUNTY LIBRARIES

CASTLETYMON BRANCH LIBRARY
TO RENEW ANY ITEM TEL: 452 4888
OR ONLINE AT www.southdublinlibraries.ie

Items should be returned on or before the last date below. Fines, as displayed in the Library, will be charged on overdue items.

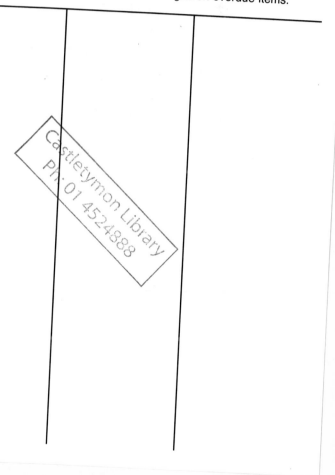

Ballpoint Press

*This book is dedicated to my wife Patricia
for her patience and support as I head to training
three times a week with Wicklow or while I spend
countless hours clocking up miles either preparing
for or participating in some marathon or other.*

Published in 2016 by Ballpoint Press
4 Wyndham Park, Bray, Co Wicklow, Republic of Ireland.
Telephone: 00353 86 821 7631
Email: ballpointpress1@gmail.com
Web: www.ballpointpress.ie

ISBN 978-0-9932892-9-3

While every effort has been made to ensure the accuracy of
all information contained in this book, neither the author
nor the publisher accepts liability for any errors or omissions made.

Book design and production by Joe Coyle Media&Design,
joecoyledesign@gmail.com

Front cover photograph by Dave Barrett.
Back cover photograph by Ciarán Byrne.

Printed and bound by GraphyCems

Contents

About The Author

CIARÁN BYRNE is a national school teacher who has never been a member of a GAA club. A keen marathon runner with over 120 finishes, the Dublin-born Wicklow resident didn't realise he was undertaking his greatest marathon challenge when he began this project on Gaelic football's most successful and enduring manager.

Acknowledgements

THE difficulty I have with thanking people who have helped me is that I always run the risk of omitting someone. If I have done so please forgive me, but be assured that your contribution made this journey possible. Many people are introduced throughout the text and I thank them all for their contribution to this project.

I am especially indebted to Andy O'Brien who was chairman of Wicklow County Board in 2009. I also want to thank members of the county board who assisted in so many ways, especially Martin Coleman, Michael Murphy and Chris O'Connor.

I am grateful to the backroom team who welcomed me from day one and who never made me feel like an outsider: Arthur French, Kevin O'Brien, Philip McGillicuddy, and Jimmy Whittle. During this voyage I got to know the late Peter Keogh. 'Uncle Peter' would loved to have seen the finished product but I know he kept a keen eye from above on what we've produced. He gave me endless encouragement and advice and for that I will be eternally grateful to the man who Mr Wicklow GAA.

Thanks to Dave Barrett who provided the photographs for the covers and elsewhere. (Unless stated otherwise, all photographs are my own.)

This journey began in 2009 and was to be published that same year but for various reasons did not happen. It was my editor PJ Cunningham of Ballpoint Press who suggested to me that I should consider publishing *A Year in Wicklow with Micko* to mark Micko's 80th birthday.

It would not have been possible to do this without the assistance of Trevor Musgrave of ONYX CONCEPT Bespoke Automotive Ltd whose sponsorship made this possible.

I also wish to thank the players and members of the panel, past and present, who welcomed me and made my journey such a voyage of discovery. If there are any errors in the text please forgive me.

Finally I want to thank Micko, a man who broke many a Dubliner's heart over many decades and with three counties. Micko, you are one of life's rare gems and it has been an honour and a privilege to have been able to shadow you for a full season.

For the wonderful five years that you gave Wicklow, but especially for 2009, go raibh míle, míle maith agat.

REST IN PEACE
Peter Keogh, 1929 – 2016

One of the first Gaels whom I met when I moved to Wicklow was the late Peter Keogh. The occasion was a Cumann na mBunscol quiz in Lawless' Hotel Aughrim. Peter was there with his notebook recording details for his Keogh's Corner column in The Wicklow People. Over the years I had the good fortune to get to know Peter. In subsequent years we used to sit beside each other on the bus journey to away matches where he would entertain, amuse and educate me with his encyclopaedic knowledge of the GAA. When I undertook this project Peter was always there to give advice and lend his support. It is my one regret that Peter is not here to see the finished product. Sonas síoraí air.

Ciarán Jones, 1986 – 2011

Garda Ciarán Jones of the Kilbride GAA Club was a member of the Wicklow senior football panel for a number of years. It was a privilege to have known him. In October 2011 Ciarán was tragically killed near his home when he was swept into the swollen waters of the River Liffey as he came to the assistance of some motorists who were stranded in torrential rain. Ciarán was off duty at the time. Ar dheis Dé go raibh a anam.

The Magic Of Micko Begins

AFTER Mick O'Dwyer's well-publicised appointment as Wicklow Senior Football Manager some months earlier, it was on a cold, damp Saturday afternoon in January in Aughrim that the GAA followers finally got to see if the Maestro of Waterville could weave his magic in the Garden County.

Over 2,500 supporters descended on the county grounds that day to see a local derby between Wicklow and neighbours Carlow in the O'Byrne Cup. Wicklow were behind for much of the match, but a late goal sealed a famous home victory. Not only that but the game was shown live on TV, only the second time in Wicklow GAA history.

I had read books on different teams and sports people over the years. Inevitably these were stories of successful teams and players. These often got me wondering what it would be really like on the inside.

With the arrival of Micko, Wicklow GAA suddenly became the centre of attention. This was not surprising. After all Wicklow, a division four team, one of only two that had never won a senior provincial title were now being managed by a man who had won provincial titles with three different counties, not to mention his eight All Ireland titles as manager of Kerry. Could this 70-year-old legend work a mircale among the Wicklow hills?

After two years of the Micko era, I approached the then chairman of the county board, Andy O'Brien, to ask if I could document in words and pictures the story of Wicklow football in

2009. Andy approached Micko on my behalf and the manager said he had no objections. And so it was that in early January 2009, I began a journey that I will never forget.

Little did I know then when this journey began that I would be part of the Wicklow set-up seven years later. After completing my reporting task, I 'inherited' a new role within the backroom team. Since 2010 I have looked after the kit and whatever logistics that have been needed to ferry equipment and personnel around to matches.

Micko lit the flame for me as he did for so many others and I am eternally grateful to him for giving me such access to him during his tenure in Wicklow.

I think it is only fitting to coincide with his 80th birthday in June 2016 that this book about his exploits as manager here in the never to be forgotten year of 2009 is finally published.

Ciarán Byrne
June 2016

CHAPTER ONE

What Have I Undertaken?

THURSDAY 8TH JANUARY
Training, Rathnew GAA Club

MY first night to attend training: as I approached Rathnew GAA Grounds I am wondering How did I find myself attending a county senior football training session and I not even a member of a club? Was this such a good idea after all? Had I bitten off more than I could chew? I had no need to worry – Martin Coleman, my contact welcomed me with open arms and brought me inside to meet Micko.

When Micko heard that I was a Dub, he had a good laugh. For years the wise maestro from Waterville had tormented Dublin fans with his glorious side of the 1970s and 1980s. Back then I detested everything about him and his Kerry side, but in the intervening years I grew to respect and admire the man. Now here I was sitting in the changing room with him and would be doing so at least three times a week for the next ... how many months?

I also met Arthur French for the first time. Immediately I could see the great camaraderie between Micko and Arthur. Arthur was wearing his best clerical black overcoat and was looking rather like a bishop. There was great banter between Micko and Arthur. Each gave as good as the other. All this time the players were getting togged out and ready to go outside to train.

It was a very clear but cold evening. The temperature had fallen to below zero and a hard frost was already setting in. The panel was running sets of three laps and Kevin O'Brien was doing stretching sessions between the laps. The players were encouraged to drink water during the intervals. Micko is the manager and there are three selectors: Arthur French, Philip McGillicuddy and Kevin O'Brien. Jimmy Whittle is the kit man. Martin Lott looks after the water and Martin Coleman is the senior team administrator.

The running began at 7.30 p.m. and lasted for about 40 minutes. Before leaving the field Micko spoke briefly to the panel about the upcoming O'Byrne Cup match against Dublin. He encouraged them to enjoy their football and that the result was not important. Dublin, despite all the hype that surrounds them are just another team and Wicklow have players equally as good as anyone Dublin have. He encouraged the players to shoot for scores. No one would give out to them if they ballooned the ball wide, but "a mortal sin" is to send the ball into the goalkeeper's arms.

There followed about 45 minutes gym work. When finished the players were given a meal of beef casserole and/or bread, cold meats, tea, water and yoghurt. Players who were unable to train either attended the session to lend their support or had a session with the physio. Pádraig Higgins, who broke his leg in October during the replayed county final between St. Patrick's and Kiltegan, received word that day that he may not be fully fit again for another three months. He hopes that the doctor was giving him a worst possible case scenario. At the moment Pádraig is able to do some straight-line jogging, and hopes that he can be back to full training in two months.

Reports in the newspapers, both local and national, are speculating that Thomas Walsh is about to return to his native Carlow. Nothing has been confirmed yet, but it appears that he may be about to lose his job and that this is weighing heavily on him. John McGrath, who had a great game in the first round of the O'Byrne Cup and who had the distinction of being the first Wicklowman to be sent off on a yellow card under the new rules, received notification the following day that he was to be made redundant. Full-back, Damian Power, who is recovering from injury, had to go on the dole for the first time in his life for a few weeks before Christmas. The recession that is following the years of the Celtic Tiger is certainly being felt among members of the Wicklow football panel.

SUNDAY 11TH JANUARY
O'Byrne Cup Second Round, Parnell Park
Dublin 0-6 Wicklow 0-9

The squad met up at 11.0 a.m. in the Glenview Hotel. They were given a meal of chicken pasta. Micko, Arthur French and Peter Keogh had porridge. Arthur was not too pleased with his serving: porridge, he said, should be made with water and not milk. Micko was inclined to agree with him. Porridge, he said, "was putting the right food into the body".

"Why are Wicklow where they are?" Peter Keogh, President of Wicklow GAA wondered. Wicklow were one of the first counties to organise themselves following the establishment of the GAA in 1884. Ashford and Roundwood, it is now accepted, were the first clubs to be established in the country. Why has there been not more progress at county level? He felt that Wicklow has always been a club-orientated county, unlike some of the more successful counties. The club comes first. Peter recallsed the former Donard midfielder Jim Rogers, who, as a garda was stationed in Offaly. Club rivalry is intense in Offaly, but when the county called, differences were put aside in the cause of the county. With the arrival of Micko, Wicklow has tasted success, a success that is beginning to transcend club rivalry.

The team talk was given in the Glenview. "If you beat Dublin you've achieved everything." Thus began Micko's team talk. He stressed that this was not an important game. It was merely an O'Byrne Cup match, but that it was important to do well. "Put your lives on the line!" he encouraged. Players look on in awe at Dublin. "What have they got? Two hands and two legs! What's so different about them? What makes them superior to us?" Although the Dublin team consisted of mainly U-21 players, some of them would be sure to feature during the league and championship. A few of the established Dublin players are nearing the end of their playing days and will have to make way for the younger men. Some of those replacements will be lining out against Wicklow today.

For every game the manager is looking for total commitment. "I don't want to see players pulling out. Look around and you'll be hurt. Shoot to score. Hit hard". If you shoot and it goes wide that's alright, but kicking the ball into the goalkeeper's arms is a disaster. It's better to pass to a player in a more favourable position. Move back to get the ball. Go looking for the ball. The ball won't come looking for you. The wind will be a factor today. Half forwards are to move back. Before you receive the ball look up and see who you will pass it to. Scan as you receive the ball. Get the ball into your chest and pass. Tackle! No giving out to one another. Encourage! If you are selected to play today it is because you are the best at the moment."

Leighton Glynn was announced as captain for the season. "Frees will be taken by Tony Hannon, left and right. Look confident and get the majority of them. When you tackle, tackle the ball not the man. Arms spread wide and get close to your opponent. Tackle the ball. Tackling the man will result in a yellow card (a sending off offence under the experimental rules). Play like demons – from the heart. Get straight into it from the start. Block with your hands. Keep your eyes open and look at the ball. Hand-eye co-ordination is vital. Practice on your own in a handball court. Train your eyes. All players are to be at training. But May 24th is the target.

The 70s Kerry team were located all over Ireland. Paídí Ó Sé never missed a training session when he was a trainee garda in Templemore. He made the 150 mile round trip from Templemore to Kerry for training. County training is two nights a week but players are expected to train three or four nights by themselves or with their club. You should be striving to kick between 150 and 200 balls at every training session. Wicklow have a favourable draw in the championship.

"How the members of the back-room team would love to be playing still. Sure it's only five years of your life. Leave the women alone. What's five years out of seventy or seventy-five? You'll have plenty of time for the women afterwards. Listen lads, booze is a joke. I've had 72 years without booze and I've had some wonderful times. Go around the county and kick ball with each other. If any player has any difficulties talk to Arthur. You'll recognise him by the shiny top of his head!"

Arthur recalled an occasion from the past when he and Micko were going to a match in Croke Park. They were staying in a well-known Dublin hotel when the general manager noticed Micko. He insisted that Arthur and Micko dine courtesy of the hotel upon their return from the match. And dine they did! A fantastic meal was placed before them and they were attended to admirably by the waiting staff. Arthur was so impress that all of this was on the house that he took out his wallet to leave a generous tip. Just then his phone rang and he left the table to get better reception. During his absence Micko picked up Arthur's wallet and called the waiting staff over one by one in order to give them a paper tip. The staff were delighted (and assumed that it was Micko who was paying). Arthur recalls that Micko was as generous with Arthur's money as if he were giving out snuff at a wake. The Kerryman and the Mayoman spar off each other in constant good-humoured banter. This camaraderie rubs off on the whole panel and backroom team. This is how real team spirit is nurtured and developed.

There was a Garda motorcycle escort for the bus from The Glenview to Parnell Park. Four members of the Garda Traffic Corp were assigned to this duty. As we left the hotel as one outrider stopped the traffic on the inside lane of the N11 as the bus joined the main road. The first car stopped at the garda's signal as did the second. I noticed a third car travelling at speed and I thought it was in the outer lane. However I suddenly realised that it was between both lanes and suddenly it collided with car number two, which in turn was pushed into car number one. What a start to the day! There were no serious injuries and assistance was called for.

I remarked to Martin Coleman that it must give a great boost to the players when they see this celebrity treatment. He said that it certainly eases the tension of all – will we get there in time? Will there be traffic congestion? Garda escorts have been a feature of Wicklow team buses since the arrival of Micko. It was through a contact Arthur had that Martin is able to arrange the motorcycle escorts.

As a motorcyclist I like to observe other motorcyclists. It is easy to see who has been trained and who hasn't. Each garda rider has reached the RoSPA (Royal Society for the Prevention of Accidents) gold standard, at least, which is the highest standard a civilian can achieve. Watching the escort work was an amazing experience. It seemed to me that this is how the team worked: Bike number four stayed in front of the team bus for the entire journey. Bike number one would peel away at a junction and stop the traffic. At a double, treble or busy junction bikes two and three would peel away. As soon as the bus would have passed through the junction the last bike would overtake the bus and fall into the number three position. To see the garda team in action was akin to watching a very well rehearsed ballet. The journey from The Glenview to Parnell was completed in twenty-five minutes. Speaking to some of the management team afterwards, the opinion is that this way of travelling to matches does wonders for the morale of the team, especially the younger members of the panel.

In the dressing-room Arthur encouraged the players to breath through their noses. This helps to ease the nerves. Paul Earls was already in there, not having travelled on the bus. In fact he had come straight from Dublin Airport from Wales where he is attending college. Term started last Monday and the workload is quite heavy. After the game he'll be flying back. The players went out for a warm-up. The weather was wet with a biting wind blowing. Certainly an O'Byrne Cup match on a January day is a far cry from the glamour of a big Croke Park championship tie. Jimmy Whittle distributed the jerseys as per the numbers in the match programme. Each player was applauded as he received his jersey. They were representing their county, the highest honour in Gaelic football. Those who were not on the starting fifteen were to wear training tops. All were to be uniformly attired.

Micko did not say much in the changing room. He told the players to go out and to play, to enjoy the game. Play well and give it 100 per cent. It does not matter if this is not the first-choice Dublin team. Many of these players will be fighting for their places on the Dublin senior team later on in the year and will want to impress Pat Gilroy and his selectors.

The first half went in Wicklow's favour; we were three points up by half time. As we sat in the changing room at half time I was surprised that Micko was not present. Jimmy Whittle was the only member of the backroom team there. He spoke to the team and stressed the importance of keeping it nice and steady. Jimmy reminded the team that this was just the first step on a long journey. Leighton Glynn emphasised the importance of upping the work rate. The crowd was against us so we had to up the work rate. Look out for each other. Laois did it as did Westmeath. It was now Wicklow's time to win their first Leinster title. No Wicklow man has a Leinster senior medal. We will be the first. There are 35 minutes left. We need man-for-man marking. We are all leaders on the field. The first minute of the game is equally important as the last. In the past Wicklow teams did not take tackles: now they do. Jimmy stressed the importance of "chasing the unlikely" – they are the scores that count.

Micko then entered the dressing room and echoed Leighton's sentiments about the work rate. It was important to encourage each other. "For God's sake lads, don't be trying to do the impossible!" We had only conceded two points in the first half and a lot of that had to do with the great blocking of the ball.

Wicklow dug deep and despite the Dubs' best efforts, stayed ahead. At the final whistle there was much jubilation. Wicklow had beaten Dublin. Ok, it may not have been a full-strength Dublin side, but let's not forget that Wicklow were far from full strength too. Dublin were playing an U-21 side but Wicklow had a fair number of young players too. True, it was only a second round O'Byrne Cup tie in January, but each little victory works wonders for the self esteem and confidence of a team. The next outing was away to Louth in Drogheda the following Sunday. There would be no garda escort back to The Glenview Hotel, but nobody minded. Not after a victory like that.

TUESDAY 13TH JANUARY
Training, Baltinglass GAA Club

It is another cold evening with a frost setting in. There are clear skies and a bright moon. Twenty-two players are at training. There are injuries and some players are out of the country. Paul Earls is in college in Wales and James Stafford is in Australia. Johnny Kinch is abroad on holidays. Paddy Dalton and Damian Power are on the pitch looking at training. Again it's sets of three laps of the field followed by some stretching exercises under the supervision of Kevin O'Brien.

Darren Hayden is by far the fastest player and simply takes off at the start of the third lap each time. Others try to keep up with him but by the final session he is a couple of seconds ahead of everyone else. Following the session on the field it is time to go indoors to do some circuit training with the weights. Each exercise lasts two minutes with a short rest period in between. Bicep curls, sit ups, press ups and medicine ball drills form the core of the gym work. Jimmy Whittle keeps a sharp eye on the stop watch while Kevin O'Brien circulates among his charges. Micko is watching and observing. Kevin does some bench presses too.

Fellas are pushing themselves and water is consumed regularly. A notable absentee is Thomas Walsh.

The Wicklow People reports that he has returned to work on the family farm in Fenagh and that new Carlow manager, Luke Dempsey, has had discussions with him. Carlow County Board will welcome him back with open arms. When he transferred to Wicklow in 2007 there was a some bad feeling between the two county boards. Thomas is playing rugby with a local club at the moment, fuelling speculation that his departure from Wicklow is imminent. Philip MacGillicuddy and some of the back-room staff are to meet him later on this week.

Micko is quoted in the local press as saying that they are trying to fix him up with a job and that a return to Wicklow is a distinct possibility. When asked if this affair is having an unsettling effect on the panel, Philip MacGillicuddy said that the lads would welcome him back. However footballers are selfish and they are all fighting for their place on the team too.

At end of the gym session the players are invited to do some chin-ups. The banter is fantastic among the squad as each player tries to set the record. Eleven is the starting point but this slowly increases. Some players need a chair to reach the overhead bar and this is noticeably absent when Billy Norman, also knows as "Little Billy", steps up to the bar. It's almost a case of having to extend the height of the bar.

Ciarán Hyland comes in for some slagging with comments to the effect that prison officers used to be much stronger. Nineteen is the record on this particular night and thus ends the session. Kevin reminds the panel that when they first started chin-ups two years ago, players were just about able to manage two or three. Progress has been excellent.

And so another winter's evening training ends. Peter Keogh is present in the gym. One can see how proud he is of his beloved Wicklow. His dilemma is whether to go to Drogheda with the footballers or go and watch the hurlers who are also in action in the Keogh Cup this weekend. The temperature is below zero as the panel leave Baltinglass. Tonight the players from the west do not have to negotiate the Wicklow Gap.

THURSDAY 15TH JANUARY
Training, Rathnew GAA Club

Twenty-two players participated in this all-gym session. There were two parts to the session and the players were divided into two groups. One group did weight lifting while the other group did paired-drills with the medicine ball. After about 40 minutes they swapped around. This session was not for the faint-hearted. Some of the medicine ball drills included hitting your partner in the stomach area with the ball for thirty-seconds.

Another dreaded exercise was the paired press-ups with one hand on the medicine ball and the other on the floor. After one press up the player passed the ball to his partner who did likewise. Two minutes of this and one would have to be digging deep into the reserves of strength and stamina. As usual the physiotherapy team was working on the injured in what is affectionately known as "Accident and Emergency".

Following the night's gym session the players had a meal of shepherd's pie with boiled potatoes, salads, yoghurt, tea, water and bread.

SUNDAY 18TH JANUARY
O'Byrne Cup Quarter Final, Drogheda
Louth 2-19 Wicklow 1-10

Twenty-six players assembled at the Green Isle Hotel on the Naas Road. Some players had already been picked up in Wicklow and at the Glenview Hotel. The panel was in good form but there was disappointment that the vocational schools side, a team that has traditionally done well for Wicklow over the years, had been beaten the previous day away to Kildare by just one point.

Weather conditions were atrocious and the Wicklow side

really threw it away with some silly errors. There are just three weeks to go until the first round of the U-21 championship. This is a straight knock-out competition. Two nights previously there was a challenge match against Meath and Wicklow were beaten by a goal.

The pre-match meal consisted of chicken pasta, water and tea or coffee after which Martin Coleman, Micko, Philip MacGillicuddy and Arthur went into session. The team sheet started off with the names of the team that beat Dublin in the previous round but some changes would have to be made. Paul Earls was suffering from a stomach bug and could not travel.

Each position and player's merits were examined and discussed. Various options were put forward and possible selections were talked about. Some of the selectors noted that it is impossible to see everything at a game and that it is vital to look at the match video. What was interesting to note is that no one selector dominated the discussion. Each gave his opinion and the final selection was one reached by consensus. The selectors are looking towards May and all roads are leading to the first round of the championship.

There was uncertainty surrounding the new rules, and in particular the yellow card rulings. However there had been a meeting during the week at which certain clarifications were made. Ironically it is the Louth manager, Eamonn MacEneaney, who is the Leinster representative on this committee. It seems that yellow cards are cumulative and if a player is yellow carded for a second time that there is a two week suspension period from the time of the second card. With regard to third and subsequent cards there is uncertainty. Suspensions are for matches in the same grade.

However a county player who is sent off on a yellow card in a Sigerson Cup match can still play for the county because of the difference in grade of competition. With the league fast approaching, two week suspensions will start taking their toll on teams.

Micko gave a short team talk before the team boarded the bus. He warned about yellow cards: Jersey-pulling, pulling with the hands and that late tackles would be punished with a yellow card. The team was more-or-less the same as last week's, but Wayne Callaghan would be starting his first inter-county game at senior level. "Go for the ball with your eyes open. If you can't catch the ball cleanly break it down." Padge McWalter was encouraged to play as he did against Dublin. "Loose play won't be tolerated. Don't be pulling out of tackles. When the ball is in the air it is a 50-50 ball. Tony Hannon is to take the frees and Séanie Furlong will take over if necessary. Play from here," Micko encouraged pounding his chest. "Don't pull out. For God's sake play for each other. Have a go. Don't kick it into the goalkeeper."

Going out to the bus I asked if there was always as much equipment and files brought to matches. Martin Coleman replied: "If Micko asks for it you'd better have it!" All players and mentors were on the bus waiting to depart for Drogheda but there was a delay ... Arthur was on the phone and Arthur is one man who will not be put out. But it is all in good humour and adds to the happy spirit in the camp.

So the bus rolled out of the Green Isle at about 12.30 p.m. The weather was quite blustery with rain forecast. Racing at Fairyhouse had been cancelled because of snow.

Today there was no garda motorbike escort.

It took about an hour to get to the pitch in Drogheda. Weather conditions were unwelcoming – a stiff cold breeze was swirling across the pitch and there was moisture in the air. In the changing rooms Micko spoke briefly to the panel. Express yourself was what he urged. The weather conditions are the same for both teams. He was looking for 100 per cent commitment from everyone. Wing forwards are to drop back and help the defence. Help one another. If you have the ball, look for a better-placed player. Don't be afraid to have a shot, but don't under any circumstances be dropping it into the goalkeeper. This is a young Wicklow side. There is no pressure on anyone. Go out and enjoy the game. Leighton, lead them out.

Louth were out of the blocks with lightening pace. They got some early scores and were in control of the game. Just before half-time Wicklow got a goal against the run of play. By half-time arrived the teams were level. A few hardy souls had made the journey from Wicklow and it was uplifting as the team entered the tunnel to hear the cheers of encouragement.

Louth 2-19, Wicklow 1-10: Wicklow's O'Byrne Cup journey hit the buffers with a bang at Drogheda on Sunday. (Peter Keogh)

After a promising first-half Micko's men were out-paced and out-played by a flying home side in the second session and were a well beaten team at the end. However, Micko appeared more perturbed at losing his promising full-forward Seánie Furlong to a red card than he was about losing the match. Should the Kiltegan star get a month, as appears likely, he will miss Wicklow's league opener against Antrim and at least their second match against Waterford, something that the manager could well do without at this stage.

The Wicklow team that lost to Louth was: Mervin Travers, Ciarán Hyland, Alan Byrne, Wayne O'Callaghan, Padge McWater (0-1), Eoin Keogh, Leighton Glynn (0-1), Patrick Brophy, Tony Hannon (0-3), Anthony McLoughlin, John McGrath, Darren Hayden (0-1), Dean Odlum (1-1), Seánie Furlong (0-2), Dean Siney. Subs. – Jacko Dalton for Wayne O'Callaghan (yellow), Seánie Kinsella (0-1) for Anthony McLoughlin.

TUESDAY 20TH JANUARY
Training at Annacurra and Awards in Dublin
Training took place on Tuesday night in Annacurra. The weather

was neither too cold nor too wet for a chanage. Meanwhile Séanie Furlong was receiving his Jury's Sports Star of the Week Award in Dublin. Travelling with Séanie was Peter Keogh. This function was a black-tie affair by invite only. The President had neither an invite nor formal dresswear. However he did manage to make it to the banquet and ended sitting with the former presidents of the GAA. Not only that but he managed to organise overnight accommodation in the hotel too. It was Wednesday afternoon before the President and Seánie made it back to Wicklow.

THURSDAY 22ND JANUARY
Training in Baltinglass

Kevin O'Brien was and is Wicklow's sole winner of an All Star Award. This is not strictly true according to Jimmy Whittle. In 1963 there was an award scheme called the Cúchulain Awards. Wicklowman Andy Philips was selected on this forerunner of what we now know as the All Stars.

Not only is this a first for the Garden County, but Andy holds a unique double distinction: he played in goal in the first floodlit match in Ireland when Bohemians played Shelbourne, a feat in itself as it was during the era of "the ban." He also played in goal on the Leinster team in a Railway Cup final – the first Railway Cup to be televised and in front of an attendance of 62,000.

Training tonight was described as something akin to riding a bicycle without a mudguard. Weather conditions were quite wet and the training surface was far from ideal. At the height of the championship we see teams play for 70 minutes on what we hope is a fine day on a good solid surface.

What is not seen are the many hours of hard slog in cold, wet windy conditions in January. This is where the real dedication and love for the game are seen – far from the glamour of the big match day without reporters, press photographers and the television cameras.

This is not the Tyrones or Dublins or Kerrys who always

seem to be there or thereabouts at the cutting-edge of the championship. Yet this is where many a player who aspires to those heights will be found on the darkest and coldest nights of January. It would serve many an armchair critic to witness a winter's training session before condemning a player for an error on the pitch in the heat of a major championship game.

The running was once again led by Darren Hayden. During each session of the laps of the field you could almost feel the effort he was making to hold back. On each final lap he would just take off and leave the rest of the panel behind. A few brave souls would try to keep up with him, but Darren just seems to be a natural athlete.

Don Jackman returned to training this evening – he was finding the running tough going but he kept at it. Another player who finds the running tough going is first choice goalkeeper Mervyn Travers. Netminders do not need to be the fastest players on a team and you could question why a net minder should do laps of the pitch. Mervyn is part of the team and if it is necessary for the rest of the panel to run laps Mervyn will do the same as his team mates.

Afterwards, the weights session lasted about 45 minutes and by nine o'clock training the team had their post training meal. Tonight the main course was rice with beef, a welcome repast for tired and weary bodies.

SUNDAY 24TH JANUARY
Challenge Match v Wicklow U-21s, Blessington

With just two weeks to go until the U-21s first round match in the championship, Philip MacGillicuddy was anxious to give his youngsters a good run-out at Blessington GAA Club. The match against the seniors was due to start at eleven. Although it was a clear bright morning with blue skies, there was a bitterly cold wind blowing. Dave Barrett was on hand with his camera to capture the action for his 125 commerorative book.

In the dressing room before the game, Jimmy Whittle took a pair of boots out of the kit bag. One of the players had left his boots behind him after Thursday's training session. A grateful John McGrath admitted that he had left his pair behind. It was remarked that the boots had never been as clean since the day they were bought.

Micko addressed the panel before the game. He encouraged the players to think of Antrim in Casement in the first round of the National Football League the following Sunday. He encouraged them to "give it a lash". If Wicklow could get a result in Belfast the next two matches are at home to Waterford and away to Kilkenny. They are two games that Wicklow should win. If they could beat Antrim first that would set us up nicely for the second half of the league and the first round of the championship would not be too long after that.

The practice match was a worthwhile exercise. Some of the younger members of the senior panel are still U-21. Within 30 seconds of the throw-in the seniors had found the back of the net. By half-time Don Jackman and Billy Norman replaced Tony Hannon and Mervyn Travers respectivelly. It was a lively contest but the seniors were in control. During the final quarter the U-21s put over some delightful points, but by then, the seniors were coasting.

Leighton scored a peach of a goal towards the end of the match. He carried the ball from his own half, laid on a pass, continued on his run past the full back and received the ball with only the keeper to beat. He then chipped the ball over the head of the advancing goalkeeper and it it seemed to linger in the air in almost a slow-motion like way before dipping under the crossbar.

The final score was 3-19 to 1-13. There has still been no news of Thomas Walsh. Walshie and Stafford were a formidable pairing and their absence would be sorely felt. Ciarán Hyland was unable to participate – he was smothered with a cold. However he did turn up to lend support when many another player would have stayed in bed.

TUESDAY 26TH JANUARY
Training, Knockananna

I had been to Knockananna once before, but that had been on a bright summer's evening some years ago. On this occasion it was a pitch black night at the end of January. One consolation was that the night was really mild in comparison to recent weeks. It was also dry.

The Knockananna pitch has a slight slope on it going from one sideline to the other. I remarked on this but was told that a lot of work had been put into the pitch over the years. At one time, while standing at one goal your eye would be level with the crossbar at the other end. But the surface of the pitch is what mattered tonight.

Whatever about the slope, exaggerated or not, it drains extremely well no matter how heavy the rain and it does not cut up – a firm surface for playing football. And playing footbal is what tonight's trainig was all about. True there were a few warm-up laps followed by stretching, but the emphasis tonight was to be on football. During the week before a match Micko likes to ease off on the heavy physical training and play football.

Tonight the U-21 were not training with the senior team and there was lots of space on the pich for running. A condition of this practice match was that a player had to punch a score if inside 30 metres. Outside of this scores could be kicked. Apart from encouraging punched scores from closer in there was a very practical reason too – to cut down on the number of footballs that would end up lost in the darkness of the fields behind the goals. Such is the romance winter training!

There is a small covered area just adjoining the changing rooms in Knockananna. This serves as a dugout cum stand. Micko sits on one of the benches. His constant call to players was "over the bar" whenever a player had any space within shooting distance. Sometimes I wonder if players are afraid to have a shot. They sometimes carry the ball closer to the goal to be surer of scoring and how many times do they over-carry, run into trouble or end up being dispossessed? Listening to Micko tonight I felt somewhat justified.

THURSDAY 29TH JANUARY
Training, Roundwood

An Tóchar GAA club is the club of Roundwood, the village that claims to have the highest pub in Ireland. It is also the home club of senior selector and manager of the county U-21 side, Philip MacGillicuddy.

Weatherwise this was a brutal night. The rain was teeming down and there was not a sign of it easing. The outfield players were doing warm-up laps when I arrived. I noticed that there seemed to be amore urgency about them tonight. They were staying together better as a group than I had witnessed up until this. The pace was noticably faster. Two players who were not running tonight were "Little Billy" and Mervyn Travers, who were going through some goalkeeping routines.

Following the few laps under the supervision of Kevin, Micko called the panel together and got them to practice taking shots at goal. After 10 minutes of this they then took shots at the other goal. It was simple ball work. A couple of days before a big match Micko does not want a heavy training session. Ciarán Hyland was back training tonight. Rory Nolan is still out injured, but he was doing some gentle jogging around the pitch. You could see that he was itching to get back playing football. But injuries must be respected.

Paddy Dalton is still unable to train. He's out since last November with a groin injury. Three years ago he had an operation on the groin. In 2008 he came on during the second half of the Tommy Murphy Cup final. He played club football since then until the injury flared up again some months ago. He tells me that it's frustrating not being able to train but that nevertheless it is important to come to the training sessions. He is doing some gym work and treadmill exercise but he would prefer "real training".

After the shooting session the panel was called together in the stand. The manager asks them if they are happy and there is a general consensus that everyone is happy. Martin Coleman outlines the arrangements for Sunday's opening round of the league. There wil be three pick up points: 9.10 a.m. at The Grand Hotel in Wicklow, 9.30 a.m. at The Glenview and arriving for breakfast at ten o'clock at The Green Isle Hotel. Breakfast was going to be chicken pasta and this is greeted with silence.

Billy Norman says that eating chicken pasta at 10 in the morning is a little heavy. Micko takes this on board and asks what Billy would like. The reserve goalkeeper says that he would prefer something lighter, maybe scrambled egg and toast. So Martin Coleman is instructed to make the necessary arrangements for Billy. When Micko asks is everyone happy with that there is a chorous of applications for scrambled egg –the concept of "Billy's Breakfast" had been born.

The team will not be eating again until after the match at about 5.30 p.m in The Carrickdale Hotel. It's a long journey on the bus so it is decided that there will be fruit provided for the journey. Jimmy Whittle is invited to give his instructions for the day: we all travel the same – navy tracksuits. "Travel as unit on the bus, off the bus, on the field and home again." Over time I realize that this something upon which Jimmy will always insist. The training session comes to an end and the players get cleaned up before having their post match meal – chicken pasta.

My first month with the Wicklow senior football team and Micko is coming to an end. So far it has been an interesting start – victory over my native Dublin and a defeat to Louth, training sessions on pitches in villages where I have never been. Far from being a rigid regimental outfit what I have experienced so far is nothing but acceptance and a warm welcome. I am treated by both players and back room staff as one of the lads. If this continues I am going to have a huge insight into the inner workings of a county team. Roll on the spring and the national league.

CHAPTER TWO

Anois Teacht An Earraigh...

SUNDAY 1ST FEBRUARY
Allianz National Football League Division Four,
First Round, Casement Park
Antrim 0-15 Wicklow 3-6

The arrangements for today were that the bus would pick up players at the Grand Hotel in Wicklow Town at 9.05 a.m. The next pick-up point was the Glenview Hotel at 9.30 a.m. and the final pick up would be at the Green Isle Hotel. Most of the Wicklow Town and Bray-based players opted for the pick-up points. I also chose the Glenview and while waiting for the bus Johnny Kinch arrived. I introduced myself and he told me that he was on the U21s last year. I asked him if he found senior inter-county football much different and he said that it was a big step up. He was enjoying the experience though.

The journey to the final pick-up point was relaxed but our driver, Seán, (christened "The Silver Fox" by Martin Coleman) was under the impression that we were meeting the rest of the panel at the Red Cow Hotel. There was some amusement on the bus as we pulled into the wrong hotel.

Even at this level of organisation information received may not exactly be the information that was given. This was a minor hick-up as the two hotels are not far from each other. We arrived at the Green Isle shortly after 10.00 a.m. where most of the panel were already assembled.

At the pre-match meal consisted there was good banter among

the players and team officials. At one stage Peter Keogh left the table and returned with a copy of The Wicklow People. He presented it to Arthur French and told the assembled audience that not only was Arthur on the front and back pages of the paper, but that he appeared in it 18 times. (The reason for this was that Arthur had deputised for Micko at the Garden County GAA Awards the previous weekend.)

The selectors and Micko went into a quiet discussion about the starting fifteen. Although there had been a panel of twenty-four given for the programme, final adjustments were being made.

Micko then spoke to the panel. The team was named. He said that it was a very important game today. Antrim were at full strength and they had the Queen's University players back after the McKenna Cup. There were players on this team who were certainly capable of matching any players, and he would say that without fear of contradiction.

"But what I've seen in quite a number of you is fear. Never before have I witnessed this fear. There are at least five or six players in this panel who show fear. We call them down in our part of the country, 'a windy footballer.' We're not going to achieve anything if we have players who are pulling out of tackles, not willing to run, not willing to chase not willing to tackle. A 'windy footballer' stands back and looks.

"Forwards must move out and channel back. Half backs must go forward and the half forwards must fall back. Against Louth I saw players standing up and watching their player soloing down the field. And when they were standing they were hoping that the ball would come back up the field. That's no good lads in this game today. Half forwards must play defensively.

"These have good forwards, lads, so Jacko (Jacko Dalton) I'd like to see you in around the square fielding high balls and that sort of thing. Do you understand me? And let the ball do the work. They must chase back and harass their forwards.

"For God's sake lads, when your man has the ball chase him and harass him lads. Put pressure on him. That's most important lads. Don't give him time to settle on the ball. If he hasn't time he'll have to get rid of it and then it's anyone's ball lads.

"Paul Earls, you were looking well the last day. You might need a little bit more football. John McGrath, move back in quick and fast. Don't be hesitating on it. You played well in our last game. Come back and defend. Work the ball out of defence. Don't be kicking it aimlessly into open spaces and things like that. We want you to use every ball well.

"Now Mervyn, you have three men in front of you. Tell them when to go for a ball and all that type of thing. Give a roar. The same throughout the field. Players we want you to encourage one another throughout the field. If there's a player in a good position on the field, Jesus, give a roar at him lads. Give a shout. Go Jacko. Go whoever. We want plenty of that vocal stuff on the pitch lads.

"Listen lads, this is the National League and we want to build a team for the championship. We want to look at every player in this league and if you are playing well you'll be on this championship team. You're getting a great opportunity now to make it onto this championship team. But you're not going to make it if you don't give total commitment when you're out on the pitch. Don't be pulling out of tackles.

"In the name of God the game is so clean today. There should be no fear. I want you to go for every ball. If you stand back and pull a jersey you'll get a black or yellow card. For God's sake go in strong – the other fellow will be getting the card. Let's see a bit of fire in the team today. Tony Hannon, you're going to take all frees. If we get a penalty who'll take it? Paul Earls will take a penalty if we get one.

"Lads for the next three Sundays we should be top of this division so it's up to you fellows today. We're not missing anyone. The players we have picked today are the best in Wicklow and we believe in you. Stand up and be counted."

The journey up to Belfast was almost uneventful. Along the way it was remarked that it was St. Brigid's Day. Uncle Peter said that he would have a word with her, and county board chairman, Andy O'Brien replied: "It won't do any harm."

An abiding picture I have of Martin Coleman is of a man with a clipboard under one arm and a pencil behind the ear. I have seldom seen him without either. Traffic was moving well, but when we got to Newry the A1 was blocked. The 'Silver Fox' stopped the bus and went over to a parked patrol car. The officers stayed in the car and advised us to go into town and follow the road out.

We eventually made it through Newry and out onto the Belfast Road again. However we had lost some time and didn't arrive at the ground until 45 mins before the game. Players were anxious to get togged off and outside for a warm-up. It was my first time in Casement Park, and I was impressed by the size of the floodlights. There was terracing on three sides of the pitch and the stand had saffron coloured seating.

In the dressing-room Arthur was dispensing a brown coloured concoction. He said that it would give an energy boost. Some were sceptical, but the man from Mayo assured us that it was a natural herbal remedy. Jimmy was anxious that all players were attired the same when they went out onto the pitch. His philosophy is that we were all together and that we should all look the same. We were told that players would be allowed out for their warm-up at 2.05 p.m.

After the warm up the players reassembled in the changing rooms for some last words of advice from Micko. As usual, when a player received his jersey, there was a round of applause. The manager went through the team one more time.

"Now lads are we ready? Now lads, it's important that we take those two points today. This is a game we want to win today. The way we want you to play today is first-time football, quick and fast. You might have seen Tyrone last night. The moment they got the ball it was gone. As quick as you can. Get the ball inside to the scoring forwards quick and fast. We need two points out of this place today. Jesus lads, don't pull out of tackles. Get out there. And fight like tigers."

Antrim dominated the first half. Wicklow were sluggish and played with little interest. Even a soft penalty was missed. Antrim were then awarded a penalty and they also missed it. You could feel that the game was slipping away from Wicklow. At half time Antrim led by 0-8 to 0-3 and had the wind to come at their backs. The half time atmosphere in the dressing room was sombre to say the least.

Jimmy spoke first: "There's feck all in it. Let the ball into Seánie at speed he'll do either of two things – he'll turn and score or get a free. We're still in touch. We're quite capable of winning this. Take positives out of the negatives. Get out and dig deep and win together. That's why we've been together since September or October. That's why we want to be part of it."

Leighton then speaks as skipper. "We've still a great chance. We could be a point behind, but we're four or five points behind. Let's see what we're made of. Let's see who the footballers are now. What's letting us down today is carrying the ball. Pump the next one in. All stand up. It's a team. Make sure you don't drop the next ball. We're going to have to start to use our heads. Micko can do no more. We've got to do it ourselves."

Ciarán Hyland chips in: "Stop letting them look good, boys. Get stuck in. I'd love to be there in the second half. Get these two points and the national league is set up for us."

Paul Earls also says a few words: "That half is gone. We've won matches from further behind against better teams. Get the heads up. Go for the thirty-five minutes."

Micko then enters the dressing-room and announces some changes. "Lads, you're playing like children. I haven't seen a player dive in and block a ball. That's what commitment is all about. Midfielders, Jacko and Tony, will you go for the ball in the air? Half backs and half forwards will you watch for the breaks coming down? There hasn't been any roar from any fellow on the field! Will you try and encourage the player going for the ball. Listen lads, we've thirty-five minutes. For God's sake lads, will you die on that pitch out there?"

The second half was a different story. Although Antrim went 0-10 to 0-4 up, Wicklow scored two goals in quick succession and nearing the end of the seventy minutes were a point up. Antrim equalised and deep into injury time got a close-in free, but it went wide. A draw was a fair result. In the dressing room, the mood had completely changed. Players and mentors were ebullient.

Micko: "We wanted to win that game but it took you 35 minutes before you decided you could play. But Jesus lads, I saw you going for balls in the second half that you were standing back and looking at in the first half. It's about fire, spirit lads and you had it in the second half. It didn't matter who went off or who came on lads, but we had that fire and spirit in the second half. Lads we're playing Waterford next Saturday. We're going to have a right training session on Tuesday. Where are we having it?"

Martin Coleman: "Knockananna"

Micko: "Knockananna. Well done boys."

Paul Earls was drained after his efforts but was facing a quick taxi ride to Belfast Airport to catch a flight to Wales where he was studying. He said training by himself was tough and the demands of his course were quite severe. As the bus left Casement Park Paul was scurring away on his own.

The team stopped at The Carrickdale Hotel just across the border. Towards the end of the meal Leighton stood up and asked for silence. He told the group that today was Rasher's anniversary. Rasher (Ray Daniels) had been the goalkeeper in Micko's early days but had been injured just ahead of the successful Tommy Murphy Cup campaign in 2007. On this date last year he took ill while on a night out, was taken to hospital in Naas but died shortly afterwards. Leighton spoke about Rasher's spirit and how it was there today. Jimmy Whittle told the group how Rasher had spoken to the team after the match two years ago when Cavan had beaten Wicklow. It was his spirit out there today. Our captain had spoken and it was a moment in time. The skipper had spoken and it was time for next week to roll on.

On the way home on the bus Kevin O'Brien asked me if my experiences were as I expected. I replied that they not. What I was expecting was a regimented approach but had found a warm and friendly atmosphere where there was a great rapport between players, management and the wider back room team. Kevin's own motto is that you do not question Micko. In this day and age of scientific training methods, very few trainers would get away with doing laps as Micko does. Micko though inspires confidence.

At the moment there are six senior members of the panel missing through injury. James Stafford is working in Australia. Attempts have been made to lure him back, but the latest is that he might be heading to the States. However, when the championship comes around it is hoped to have a full-strength squad again. Kevin maintains that footballers are similar to horses. Some are good in the heavy conditions of winter football while others are much better on the drier and harder surfaces of the summer months. Some simply won't have the fitness that is required for the hard surfaces. It is fitness that has won tight games for Wicklow since Micko's arrival. In the past Wicklow would not have had anything left during the closing minutes of a tight game. That has changed. Wicklow are now able to reach depths within themselves that they never knew existed before. Today's game was a perfect example of this.

Kevin says that he would do anything that Micko asks of him, even the proverbial "stand on your head". The remainder of the journey was spent relaxing. Some players played cards at the back of the bus, some sat quietly while the rest of us chatted and reminisced on what had been a hard won national league point away from home.

TUESDAY 3RD FEBRUARY
Training, Knockananna

After four weeks of training in frost and rain, the weather finally won out. Text from Martin Coleman reads: "Training cancelled tonight. I will contact you with details for Thursday night's venue later. Martin". Yesterday the snow that was promised by the forecasters finally arrived. Depending on your location the snow arrived at different times. However, by Monday nightfall, most of Wicklow was experiencing snow of some description. On Tuesday morning both the Wicklow and Sally Gaps were impassable, and west Wicklow, in particular areas around Baltinglass and Blessington, were under a blanket of snow. Throughout the day there was a bit of a thaw with Wicklow Town being cold and wet. However the west of the county was still in the grips of the big freeze. This cancellation of training allows me to catch up on the diary.

WEDNESDAY 4TH FEBRUARY

Text from Martin Coleman: "Training in Roundwood on Thursday night. Have gear suitable for indoor training. 7.30 start, Martin". Since Monday much of the county has been in the grip of a big freeze. There were huge tailbacks on the M50 and N11 on Monday evening. Players would be expected to do their own training on occasions like this. Today the weather improved considerably, but the forecast is that the cold snap is due to return tonight.

THURSDAY 5TH FEBRUARY

The cold snap has returned. The Wicklow and Sally Gaps have once again been impassable. Some schools have not opened. In Wicklow Town snow began to about 9.30 am. By 11.0 am. there was a blanket of snow in the town. Parents were calling to take their children home from school. Roads in the town were becoming treacherous and there were reports of cars sliding into other cars. Most schools in the town decided to send their pupils home. Before midday Martin sent a text: Due to weather conditions training is now switched to Baltinglass tonight. Bring indoor training gear, Martin".

Listening to local radio while on the way home from school, the prospects of getting to west Wicklow was not inviting. I rang Martin and told him that I would not be venturing over to Baltinglass tonight. He understood my position and added that there would have been very few at training had the venue not been changed. Roundwood was impassable.

SATURDAY 6TH FEBRUARY
Allianz National Football League Division Four, Second Round, Aughrim
Wicklow 0-15 Waterford 2-9

I am in Cavan attending the AGM of Cumann na mBunscol Náisiúnta so I am unable to attend the first home game of the current league. When I eventually spoke to Martin Coleman I was able to sense his great disappointment. Peter Keogh reports:

A Wicklow team short six of the players that helped them to get a draw with Antrim in Casement Park a week earlier struggled to eke out another draw with Waterford at Aughrim on Saturday.

Micko rested the four U-21 players, Ciarán Walshe, Anthony McLoughlin, Dean Siney and Darren Hayden because of the championship against Longford the next day and he was also short of full back Stephen Kelly and full forward Seánie Furlong.

As in Belfast Micko has happy to settle for a draw but how he must be longing to have a full panel of players available to him once again. It was only by calling on three of the U-21 squad during the course of the match that he managed to get something out of this very hefty challenge from John Kiely's side. John McGrath was Wicklow's outstanding player and also finished up top scorer with 0-4.

Wicklow – Mervyn Travers, Ciarán Hyland, Alan Nolan, Alan Byrne; Padge McWalter, Eoin Keogh, Leighton Glynn (0-2); Paddy Brophy, Jacko Dalton; Paul Earls(0-3), Tony Hannon (0-3), John McGrath (0-4); Dean Odlum (0-2), Don Jackman, Jonathan Kinch. Subs – Ciarán Walshe (0-1) for Jackman (Yellow); Mick McLoughlin for Keogh; Darren Hayden for Kinch; Anthony McLoughlin for Brophy (Yellow Card).

SUNDAY 7TH FEBRUARY

Today was to be the day of the first round of the Leinster U-21 Football Championship at Pearse Park Longford. The game was called off because of the inclement weather.

TUESDAY 10TH FEBRUARY
Training, Annacurra

Originally training was scheduled for Knockananna but was changed to Annacurra. No dressing-room facilities available to the county players? What's going on? Annacurra have a fine facility. At long last Wicklow GAA has made progress. Players are valued and treated with the proper dignity that they deserve. Have we suddenly reverted back to a previous time when Wicklow football was regularly ridiculed?

I arrived in Annacurra about 7.20 for a 7.30 start. It was my first time there and I was impressed with the size of the community/GAA centre. But why was it not open to the county team? I was also surprised at what seemed to be a poor turn-out with players togging out at their cars.

Fortunately it was a mild night in comparison with what the weather had been for the last week. It was great to see Rory Nolan ready to take part in his first training session with the panel. Rory is a big addition to any team. Dara Ó hAnnaidh and Paddy Dalton were present but are still not fully fit. They will do some gym work if they can get access to the centre. Mervyn Travers is unable to train. Yesterday he had been to the doctor who gave him an injection in a troublesome knee. He must rest for a couple of days. Another member of the panel told Martin that he had received two day's work and would not be able to make training. In the early days of the recession of 2009 everyone needs whatever work they can get, whenever they can get it. Eventually the centre is opened up. As the players gathered on the pitch I sensed a different mood in the camp. This was not the happy jovial group that I had experienced on every occasion since I began following the team last month. Was this the result of the bad performance against Waterford?

Jimmy called me over to his car as I was going onto the pitch and handed me a tracksuit and polo top. He said that since I was part of them that I should look like one of them. I appreciated the gesture and I hope to wear the county colours with pride from now until the team's final outing this season... whenever that might be.

Micko called the squad together before the training began but said very little. "Lads indiscipline cost us the two points against Waterford." He insisted that his players must stop talking back to referees. "Indiscipline cost us a goal and three points two days ago. It also cost us two yellow cards. Indiscipline must be eradicated from our game." As he finished, I noticed that the local club team was also training on the other side of the pitch. Could this be really happening? Surely the county team can have a pitch to themselves. It's noticed that the squad is not as fit as it was this time last year and that players are off the pace. Next on the agenda is a series of sets of three laps. This time the players are timed and the fastest pace on the first set is 1.46. As the players are passing by the start/finish pole their time is called out. On the second set the pace has dropped back to 1.52. A big effort is called for the final set and the lads do put in the effort. They clock the fastest time of the evening at 1.37. The mood somewhat improved as the session progressed.

WEDNESDAY 11TH FEBRUARY

Mark Kennedy reported on the back page of The Wicklow People that Wicklow were in trouble over playing Seánie Furlong in the match against Antrim. Seánie had received a red card in the O'Byrne Cup defeat to Louth and there was some confusion as to whether or not cards in the provincial competitions carried over to National League matches. There was talk that the player could get a twelve week suspension if it were found out that he had been illegal in the Antrim game. In retrospect I wondered if the difference in mood had anything to do with this news. Seánie did not play against Waterford. Would this serve as his match suspension or would there be bad news for Wicklow?

THURSDAY 12TH FEBRUARY
Training, Baltinglass GAA Club
Tonight it is mild. Micko encourages the players to stick with it. "If you are not getting your game yet it's because you're not ready. Stick with it. You have a chance to play for Wicklow." He recalled that in Kerry there was one player who didn't make the team for three years, but when he did, he won three All Irelands and three All Stars. "Stick with it lads." That player was Ger Lynch.

The pitch in Baltinglass is heavy and the going is tough. But Micko encourages them to work through the pain.

There are only about twelve weeks to the the Leinster championship. He lays down a rule that no player is to talk back to a ref again. That's the Kerry policy (but Kerry lost it in '08). Don Jackman is back training. He is feeling the pace big time but sticks with it. He may be off the pace and throwing up but he finishes his laps. The mood is better than Tuesday. There's general discontent about Mark Kennedy's piece in The Wicklow People. He also maintained that Seán Mulryan of Ballymore Properties was pulling out of his sponsorship of Wicklow. Some days later Andy O'Brien, Wicklow County Board Chairman, was able to go on local radio and state that the Ballymore sponsorship of the Wicklow Team had been confirmed for another year.

SUNDAY 15TH FEBRUARY
Challenge match v U-21s, Newtown GAA Club

This was a pleasant spring morning. The mood was good – as a result of two major events. Yesterday the U-21s travelled to Pearse Park to play Longford in the Leinster Championship. It was not looking good for Wicklow with two minutes to go. They were behind by a point. Anthony McLoughlin got the ball on his own 20 metre line and went on a solo run up the pitch. He was determined to change the outcome of the game and scored a magnificent equalising point. At that stage all were expecting to have to play extra time but Wicklow went on to score another two points in injury time to record a famous victory. Wicklow hadn't played for forty minutes of the game and although the result was very satisfying the performance was far from that. Laois in Aughrim in two weeks time is next on the list. Laois will be looking for revenge for their heavy defeat to Wicklow the previous year in Portlaoise in championship. The other bit of good news was that Seánie Furlong was cleared to play. That was a relief as there was talk of one stage of a twelve week suspension. A lesson well learned.

Darragh O'Sullivan from the St. Pat's has been called into the panel and was playing very well. Garrett Doyle from Newtown played with the U-21s in the past. Garrett is a county coach and was also on the panel in the past. No doubt both men will want to make a big impression on the selectors. The game is quite competitive but the seniors, as expected, have the upper hand. Micko called the seniors together for a pep talk: "The team with the ball should be loose. They shouldn't be marking. Half backs can attack but if we lose possession ye must get back like a race horse. That's where fitness is required. Don't over attack or we will be left exposed. That happened last week. You won't catch the ball with one hand lads. If you can't catch it break it down and our half lines will clean up."

The game was much livelier than the previous challenge in

Blessington. Damian Power came on late in the first half and fielded a high ball under pressure. However the next ball that came in saw him collide with his own goalkeeper and he had to leave the field. He has hurt his shoulder. This is a big worry for the selectors – Damian is the first choice full back. At one stage the U-21s were awarded a penalty and Garrett Doyle took it. There was much disgust on the senior line with this decision. Ok Garrett got the goal from it but he's no longer under twenty-one. What if Wicklow are awarded a penalty against Laois? Who will take it then? Jimmy Whittle summed it up aptly when he said: "Sloppy in training sloppy in a game".

After the match both panels gather round their respective coaches on either side of the pitch. Micko urges: "We've got to go through the pain barrier lads. If we want to win anything we've got to go through the pain barrier. Look lads, there is no gain without pain." Training will now be three nights a week. He asks what nights would suit and after some discussion it is agreed that the nights will be Monday, Wednesday and Friday with a game on Sunday. Not all players will be able to make the three nights.

With the three week break to the next league match there is an opportunity to work on fitness.

MONDAY 17TH FEBRUARY
Training, Baltinglass GAA Club
I am away for a couple of days and am unable to make training. Why do I feel bad when I can't attend a session?

WEDNESDAY 18TH FEBRUARY
Training, Newtown GAA Club
It is a beautiful mild night. Spring has sprung and the form is good. I get a chance to talk to Martin Coleman while Micko takes charge of a game. Martin is the team administrator. It is his duty to look after the various pieces of paper and administrative work. From an independent perspective it strikes me that this

management team is a well-oiled machine. Each knows the other's role and everything appears to run smoothly. I asked about Jimmy's talk at half-time and if it was common practice to stay out of the changing room. The reason why Micko only comes into the dressing room towards the end of the half-time break is that he meets with the selectors and they discuss the performance during the first half. Jimmy takes control of the dressing room. Otherwise a strong willed player might take over and this might not be the best thing for the team. This pattern has evolved since Micko's arrival and it works. Micko has brought a whole new dimension to Wicklow, and much of it is in the little things. For example, before a recent game, Leighton asked Micko the name of the referee so that the captain could have a few words with the man in black before the toss. Little things mean a lot; the referee has a name and likes to be wished well before a game. Ironically the Seánie Furlong incident came to light during a new rules review committee meeting about yellow cards and whether John McGrath was eligible to play because he had received two yellows. Talk about getting ambushed. Perhaps one of Martin's most difficult tasks is when he has to tell a player that he is no longer needed. That is never easy.

Micko encourages the team, "Give the ball and go. Support play is vital lads. For the next thirteen weeks no beer and no cigs. I want total commitment lads. No graveyard passes. Pass it up into the air and you'll get a fella killed. No soloing and no hopping. Play the ball first time."

FRIDAY 20TH FEBRUARY
Training, Knockananna GAA Club

I didn't think that I would be able to make training tonight but I did. Well not exactly. I was late and went straight up to the Wagon Wheel pub where the team have their post-match training meal.

While having his meal tonight a young girl comes up to Micko and asks for his autograph. He is delighted to be able to oblige and when I suggest that I take their photograph he pushes his meal aside. It is moments such as this that have made the whole Micko Adventure in Wicklow so memorable for so many of all age groups.

SUNDAY 22ND FEBRUARY
Challenge Match v U-21s in Aughrim

It's a beautiful Sunday morning in the County Grounds Aughrim. There is a challenge match against the U21s who play Laois next week in the next round of the Leinster Championship. In the pre-match talk Micko stresses the importance of discipline on the pitch. Under no circumstances are players to talk to the referee. On a technical point the manager insists that players do not give away silly frees by not placing their foot under the ball for a pick-up. The game is lively with the seniors outscoring the U-21s, but it has to be said that once again, it is much more competitive and evenly matched compared to the game in Blessington some weeks previously.

Pádraig Higgins is recovering from his broken leg and has a rub-down with physical therapist Noel Molloy. He's going to do some jogging around the pitch and I join him. I feel that I will be able to keep up with him – after all I am an experienced distance runner and Pádraig is recovering from a serious injury. How naïve! I am able to reel off eight minute miles without a bother. At one stage I was capable of a sub-three hour marathon pace. On my second lap with Pádraig I realised that he was running a sub-seven minute mile pace. Wasn't I glad when he took a break after three laps.

Soon it was time for another set of three laps. By the third set I was struggling. We took a break and were joined by Paddy Dalton who was also recovering from injury. The three of us did another set of laps but by the end of the second lap I had to drop out "and do some stretching". Paddy has some good news: he passed his exams!

MONDAY 23RD FEBRUARY
Training, Baltinglass GAA Club

Players have been notified by text to be ready to start at 7.30 p.m. I am unable to attend tonight due to another commitment. It is beginning to dawn on me the huge sacrifice and demand on one's time it is to be part of a county team ...

WEDNESDAY 25TH FEBRUARY
Training, Newtown GAA Club

A mild night but there are only twenty-one players at training and four of these were on the injury list. The players spent most of the session concentrating on passing and scoring points.. The game was loosely based on backs v forwards. It was great to see goalkeeper Mervyn Travers back and at his vocal best. "Left shoulder Rory," to "he's on your right". He is constantly shouting at his team mates and even in a packed ground his voice can be heard clearly.. Jimmy Whittle is in goal for the reds and is reliving moments of his youth – much to the amusement of all. In fairness it has to be admitted that it still requires a little magic to beat him.

Kevin O'Brien is doing a light work-out with four of the recovering. He starts off with some ball drills followed by stretching. "Great to see you back. You are needed by this team," he goes. Kevin is one strong motivator – but he also participates in the training. At one stage he gets the players to pair off to do sit-ups with the ball. He gets me to stand and throw the ball to him as he does the sit-ups. He then calls for 50 and begins to count. I cannot believe the force with which he throws the ball back to me. He is also doing the counting. As soon as the sit-ups are completed he calls for 30 press-ups. Straight after that he conducts some running across the pitch at jog, half and three-quarter pace. This is followed by soloing drills in various guises. He is adamant that his recovering group will train for as long as the rest of the panel. To conclude he gets the four to jog to the 13-metre line and then to jog backwards to the end-line. It's forwards to the 20-metre line and back again. This is repeated to each line on the pitch until they reach the far goal. Back to solo drills. Kevin insists that the first three metres are vital and stressed that no players should hop or solo the ball in those first strides.

"You mightn't be able to run 20 laps but you'll be able to beat your opponent over three metres." Kevin tells them when Micko first arrived that it took three to four months for the panel to keep their heads up. "Catch the ball and keep your head up. Look around you. It's almost being like a basketball player."

The session ends with a number of sprints from the half-way to the goals and back. It was a productive session and there is the feeling of hard work done with a lot achieved. Eddie has the meal ready upstairs in the club house. Tonight being Ash Wednesday there is a fish and vegetable pie. If the team is training on Good Friday it will also be a fish dish! Some traditions will never die.

FRIDAY 28TH FEBRUARY
Training, Knockananna GAA Club

It's another mild night with a very slight mist. The numbers at training are slightly down again. Three nights a week as well as a match is a huge commitment. Seventy minutes on a summer's day from the stands and terraces give no indication as to what is required. By the time I arrive the team is doing warm-up laps. Micko then separates the squad into two groups for reds v yellows. I decide to do some running with the players who are recovering from injury. Tonight Pádraig Higgins, Stephen Kelly and Damian Power are with Kevin. God help us!

The warm up laps are not too fast – or so I think. I am pacing myself alongside Pádraig who told me that he was a little sore after Wednesday's training. I am not surprised – he was working hard. Tonight I should be able to keep up with him as he is taking it a little easier that he did on Sunday last. Eight minute mile pace will suit me fine. That was until Kevin began some ball drills and insisted that I join in. I haven't played football in years, and when

I did I was neither very skilful nor very strong. However the three lads encouraged me and so I joined in. After the passing drills we ran at three-quarter pace. Pádraig is not pushing too hard and I am able to keep up with him.

The practice match doesn't last very long and Micko calls the whole squad together for some relay races and sprints. (As our small group joins the rest of the squad, Kevin asks some teenagers who are watching the training if they'd like to have a kick around with a ball for a while. They are delighted and a simple gesture such as this really helps the team's image.) At this stage I decide to drop out. However one team is short of its fourth member and I am drafted in. Big mistake. I'm with the slower players but in my leg of the relay I am up against Padge McWalter, Ciarán Hyland and Alan Nolan – three speedsters. I am the last in each leg, but then I received the baton from Billy Norman who is not known for his turn of speed and I pass it onto the Damian Power who has an impossible task of catching the others. We don't. Micko insists that we run four legs of the relay so that we all end up where we started. At relay number four Micko decides to give me a head start so I tear off. I hear the whistle and no sooner have I reached the corner flag than I am being overtaken.

Then it happens ... tightness in the right hamstring and even more tightness in the left hamstring. I cannot show any sign of injury and so I struggle to pass the baton on to Damian. Our team is hopelessly last. It is then that I realize for the first time in my life that inter-county football is not only for young men, but for the very fit and very strong. I try to disguise my discomfort and make my way to the start area slagging my three opponents that they have no respect for their elders. I drop out and try to do a few stretches. Meanwhile the rest of the panel are doing sets of sprints across the pitch and back. Training ends after an hour. The club leagues are starting this weekend and Micko is asked if the county players can be released to play. He says that they can for this weekend, but that is all. It is particularly difficult for a club with a number of county players to field their strongest team. Is it any wonder why the club championship in the more successful counties often runs very late into the year?

CHAPTER THREE

March Of The Many Weathers

SUNDAY 1ST MARCH
Training, Baltinglass

March is going to be a busy month – about twelve weeks to go until the first round match against Longford in the Leinster Championship. There are away matches in the league to Kilkenny and Leitrim followed by home matches against London and Clare. Today is a bright blustery morning in Baltinglass. There are only twenty players present as the U-21s are in action this afternoon in Aughrim against Laois in the championship. Arthur has made his return to the fold ... after sailing around the Caribbean with some well-known business associates for a couple of weeks. He cracks a few jokes and amid much laughter and good humour the session breaks up.

In the U-21 game Laois are comfortable winners on a score line of 1-18 to 1-4. After months of training and much promise, the season is over for the younger players. With six seniors on the panel, hopes were high of progressing. The pain of the defeat is still very raw.

TUESDAY 3RD MARCH
Training, Roundwood

After a break of almost a month the Allianz National Football League is due to recommence for Wicklow on Sunday. The day is turning cold and rain is beginning to fall. By early afternoon it is quite heavy and AA Roadwatch is saying that both the Wicklow and Sally Gaps are becoming impassable. At four o'clock Martin is forced to contact the entire panel by text: Training cancelled due to weather. Training in Knockananna on Thursday night. Both gaps are impassable by 5.00 p.m. Just after a good week's training last week comes the defeat of the U-21s and now senior training can't happen because of the severe weather. Will Wicklow ever get a break?

THURSDAY 5TH MARCH
Training, Knockananna

The biting wind of earlier on today is gone and the weather is a little milder. Kevin is concerned that the players are not tuned in. "Dig in," he urges. "Those first three yards are vital!" What I have noticed about Kevin is that he is always so positive. Even when he is not satisfied with the effort that some of the panel are making, he still manages to see the positive. The drills continue with overhead and low passes, passes to the chest, passing with the strong and weak leg. The session ends with relays. Teams consist of the backs, half backs, midfielders, half forwards and full forwards. There are four races so all end up back where they started. There is an element of fun to this exercise, but there is also some competition. In many ways training reminds me of teaching a PE lesson in primary school!

The squad retire to The Wagon Wheel for the post-training meal. Spirits are high; Jimmy is picked on for wearing a Hibernian top. Jimmy retorts that some others in the present company are wearing garments from various establishments, to which Micko responds like lightening. "But all were made in Ireland ... unlike your top." Arthur tells of a super potion that he has for all the players. There are eleven weeks to go to the championship and it is no use taking it two weeks before the big game. Micko is partial to a big fry-up. "It's the tastiest thing you can have, but it's sheer poison." He then adds with the mischievous twinkle in his eye: "A little bit of poison is good now and again." He goes for second helpings of lamb casserole and says "it was Kerry lamb!"

SUNDAY 7TH MARCH
Allianz National Football League Division Four,
Third Round, Nowlan Park
Kilkenny 0-3 Wicklow 7-24

Today we meet in The Judges Baltinglass where breakfast is scrambled eggs. I am sitting beside Paddy Dalton who reckons that he is 99 per cent fit. He participated in the full training session last Thursday but felt sore afterwards. The manager does not have a whole lot to say to the team except to look out for the yellow cards. The midfielders must hold back. Scores taken today will be very important if and when scoring differences are calculated at the end of the league. He urges players to pass the ball to a better placed man. The starting fifteen will not be that which is listed in the programme.

The game is very one-sided and played in front of a very small crowd. At half time Kilkenny were scoreless and the result a foregone conclusion long before the final whistle. Next week will be a much stiffer test with a trip to Carrick-on-Shannon. By the time we are boarding the bus for home there is heavy rain falling. The post match meal is in The Springfield Hotel.

MONDAY 9TH MARCH
Training, Knockananna

The rain is hammering down as evening approaches and I find myself in Dublin. It does not look as if I will make training tonight so I ring Martin Coleman and tell him of my predicament. Martin tells me that he would ring me if anything extraordinary happened. He will also let me know what the arrangements are for the rest of the week.

As I arrived home about 10.00 p.m. Martin phoned me to tell me they were just leaving Knockananna "after a wonderful session". Nothing to do with training though. The players had left and the backroom team were getting ready to leave. Micko had already left and as Arthur was going through the door he met a local woman coming into the pub carrying a button accordion. Arthur asked if there were a session about to begin and he was told that there was. He dashed over to Micko who had already started his car and insisted that the manager go back inside for a song or two. Micko obliged, took the box, played and sang. The impromptu session lasted for about half an hour after which Micko had to leave. Of all the nights to miss!

WEDNESDAY 11TH MARCH
Training, Annacurra

Training consists of a practice match with the reds playing the yellows. Kevin plays for one of the teams to balance up the numbers. Micko is reffing and the no hopping or soloing rule is applied. Any infringement of this results in a free. There is also a moratorium on bad language. Later the ban on soloing is lifted and there are some sprints "for those who look like they might need a little bit extra." There seem to be fewer at training this evening and when I mention this Micko's attitude is, "you learn better in a small class".

Martin Coleman said watching Micko play the accordion in Knockananna was an experience. It was as if he was at home playing in his own kitchen. Such is the charisma of the man. Peter Keogh's opinion was that following this current Wicklow outfit was like being a great hurling match. "Take your eye off the ball for a second and you miss something special." Typical of my luck and not a camera in the house either!

THURSDAY 12TH MARCH
Training, Baltinglass

At last there is a noticeable stretch in the spring evening. When the clocks go forward at the end of the month there won't be many more nights training under lights. Tonight there is plenty of ball kicking – forwards and midfield trying to put it over the bar and backs clearing it upfield. There is a good atmosphere on the pitch. Paul

Cunningham (Bray Emmets) and Cathal McNicholas (Newtown) from the U-21 panel have been drafted in. Goalies Mervyn Travers and Billy Norman train separately away from the rest of the panel. Tony Hannon, although togged out, does not participate. He is resting having taken a slight knock but assures Micko that he'll be fit for Sunday's clash with Leitrim. The session is not too strenuous and the panel is called together. "We want everything in order. Treat this game like a championship match. Get a good run in. I've noticed that we're inclined to use a little bad language. I want you to cut that out. Keep one eye on the ball and one eye on the man. Now lads, this is a very important game. No parties between now and Sunday. There are thirty on the panel and I know that there are some of you who haven't got your game yet. Persevere. Look lads, you've got to work to get on the team. Look at Dean (Odlum). He wasn't getting his game but look at the condition he's in now. Be prepared to be taken off and put on. We believe you're good enough to play for Wicklow. We believe in you. I often give the example of Ger Lynch. For three years he sat on the bench, but look lads, he went on to win three All Irelands and three All Stars. Stay with it. Everyone is important. Now look lads, that's all I've got to say. We'll have a chat on Sunday."

Jimmy Whittle reminds the team of their match day attire: "We turn up as a team. We go home as a winning team." Team captain Leighton Glynn adds: "It's an important game. We have three nice games and then we'll have four wins. I want to play in Division Three next year."

There is a penalty competition with Leighton in goal. One miss and you're out is the rule. Ciarán Hyland wins. Supper consists of lasagne and so ends another week's training.

SUNDAY 15TH MARCH
Páirc Seán Mac Diarmada
Leitrim 0-13 Wicklow 0-11
At The Green Isle Hotel the sign that goes on the front of the bus

"Wicklow Senior Football Team" had been left behind. Two of the Arklow-based players were late and the story was that they didn't recognise the bus without the sign. Apparently the number seven jersey is also missing. It was suggested that Jimmy Whittle put a jersey in the window of the bus to aid identification. Jimmy was having none of that – what if another jersey were to go missing?

There was a moment when you realize what following a team can mean to someone. A young boy, Dylan, was brought onto the bus by his mother. Dylan wished to thank the team for signing a jersey that would be raffled later on in the week at a fund-raiser. He needs a serious operation in Crumlin Children's Hospital. A league game in March somehow seems somehow a little less important when compared with the health of a sick child.

We stopped in Mullingar for scrambled eggs and toast. After the food, Micko spoke briefly to the panel. "Now lads, this is our most import game since Antrim. We have injured players but we have picked the in-form players for the starting fifteen. We can't give you all games. Be patient. We'll select but we want total commitment. Ye are all part of the team. Do your very best. At home kick a ball against a wall. Kick as much ball as possible. We're not putting pressure on you. If we concede a score I don't want you putting the head down and giving out. Be out straight to your own man. Up in the air it's a 50-50 ball. Get it into the full forward line quick and fast. The three full forwards are playing well. Take your points. Goals will come. No shooting from impossible angles. We don't care who scores. Delivery is important. Half backs don't over attack. Midfield fall back. Go away from the player with the ball. Quick and fast. In training we don't allow hopping or soloing and the scores come quickly. Do that in the game. Look lads, this is a game we have to win. Put your own body out there. Eyes wide open. Block well. Harass on the double. Fall back. The quicker the better. Look lads this is preparation for 24th May."

Some players had a gentle kick around while waiting to board the bus. Tyrone are playing in Mullingar today and some supporters are in the foyer of the hotel. I meet Mark Conway and I explain what my project is about. He thinks it is a great idea. Mark was instrumental in the formation of Club Tyrone and has played a large role in the development of the strategic plans of both the GAA and Cumann na mBunscol Náisiúnta. (Westmeath almost pull of the shock of the day but are beaten in added time by the All Ireland champions.)

The rest of the bus journey is pleasant and we reach Carrick-on-Shannon about an hour before throw-in. As we walk towards the dressing rooms we are all impressed by the new stand. There are numerous plaques on the end wall of the stand. The dressing rooms are impressive – large, bright and airy. They are located under the new stand. Players change into the gear and get ready to go out onto the pitch for their warm-up.

There is a stiff breeze blowing down the pitch. The ground is fairly soft. Micko tells them not to attempt to bounce the ball – it won't come back up as the ground is so soft. Compared to last week there will be a good crowd at this game. Leitrim are also pushing for promotion from the basement division of the league. They are seeking revenge for the defeat in Aughrim in the semi-final of last year's Tommy Murphy Cup.

Back in the dressing room players receive their jerseys. There is a silence which is good. Players are focused. Leighton Glynn breaks the silence: "We're coming out of here with two points!" Micko speaks briefly: "Play direct football. Fast and quick. No hopping. Stand up and be counted. This is a game of vital importance! We must win. That's all about it. Mulligan is deadly off frees. We're giving frees away because we're using our hands. Fast and quick is most important. Give the player coming through the ball. First time football. Put your bodies on the line today. Now get out there and win!"

At half time Wicklow are trailing by three points and no one is happy in the dressing room. Jimmy has a few words with the team while the selectors deliberate outside the changing room.

"We've got the breeze this half." Ciaran Hyland says: "Toughen up. It's only three points against a strong wind." Leighton adds: "Play the ball nice and early." Jacko Dalton pipes up: "This is a championship match for us. We lose today and this year is over."

Micko then enters the dressing room. "Just relax, lads. Paddy Dalton is coming on for Darragh O'Sullivan. Leighton go half forward. Paddy go half back. Look lads, you can't hop the ball. Some of you are only looking on. You look afraid. Midfield play it in low and fast. Stay back. Our delivery is terrible. Send the ball in quick and fast. For God's sake don't open your mouth to the referee. He'll bring the ball forward. Just 35 minutes. Jesus lads, we want you to die out there. Don't hop. Quick and fast. Stand together for thirty-five minutes. Now get out there and give it everything you've got!"

The second half is much tighter and Wicklow might have won the game but lose by two points. The team is very silent trooping into the changing room. Micko comes in. "Lads, we made a few mistakes. We lost. We might have won. But look lads, it's another game in preparation for the championship. Training is in Knockananna on Wednesday night."

Not much more is said. On the way back there is a stop for a meal. As the team go into the restaurant, there is a standing ovation for Micko from the people who are in the lounge. Such is the respect that the man commands. Maybe it was not the best day in Micko's reign, but the maestro is still recognised for what he is – a man who has contested 27 All Irelands at one level or another, either as a player, selector or manager.

WEDNESDAY 18TH MARCH
Training, Knockananna

The mood is downbeat after Sunday's defeat. However it is still possible to get out of the basement division if we win our remaining games and if some of the results from other matches go our way.

Standing on the sideline I notice that one player does not seem to be fully participating in the practice match. He seems to be totally disinterested in what's going on. As one selector put it, "He's having a sulk." The practice match has not been going his way and he is feeling a little aggrieved. Eventually he leaves the pitch. When asked he says that if anyone else does anything wrong they get away with it but that he gets blown up every time.

At the end of the session Micko calls all the players together. "We made a lot of mistakes against Leitrim. We should have won. We should have been beaten by Antrim. We have to get you to mark one another. After a score mark closely. If you hop the ball you lose two seconds. That's a bad habit. Páidí Ó Sé could hop the ball because he couldn't solo! He was like a greyhound after a rabbit. Look for the loose player. We'll have two good games and a great one against Sligo. It's only nine weeks from Sunday. We might bring the scales along the next night. Some of you are a few pounds overweight. How're you feeling Seánie?"

"Great Micko!" is Seánie's reply much to the amusement of all. With that training comes to an end and the meal is in Jacob's tonight. The Wagon Wheel does not open on a Wednesday so the other hostelry in the village hosts the panel.

THURSDAY 19TH MARCH
Training, Baltinglass
I'm not at training because of a prior appointment in Dublin but I learn that the County Board was fined €400. (Jimmy Whittle, one of our Maor Uisce entered the field of play when he shouldn't have.)

SATURDAY 28TH MARCH
The Republic of Ireland played Bulgaria in Croke Park in group eight of the qualifiers for the 2010 World Cup in South Africa. Ireland take a very early lead against the Bulgarians who are without some of their star performers. However after the dream start it is backs-to-the-wall stuff as the visiting team put the home side under tremendous pressure. After 70 minutes Ireland

concede an own goal and escape with a draw. The next game is against the World Champions in Bari on Wednesday. The general feeling is that we are going to be well beaten.

SUNDAY 29TH MARCH
Aughrim
Wicklow 1-20; London 0-9

Last night Antrim beat Sligo so that puts Wicklow back in the promotion race and we need Waterford to drop some points in their remaining games. Of the original twenty-four listed in the programme, three are unavailable due to injury or illness. One player played for his club the night before. One of the selectors was infuriated by this and would like to see the club deducted two points.

In the changing room before the team went out onto the pitch, Micko spoke briefly. He stressed the importance of teamwork. "Every player is playing for Wicklow and must give 100 per cent. There can be no pulling out of tackles. Quick and fast football lads. Find a man. For God's sake don't be giving the ball away. No high tackles. We don't want any yellow cards. We want total commitment! Now get out there."

It was a bright sunny day with a slight wind blowing but very few fans had turned up. Perhaps it was because Wicklow were supposed to win this game easily enough combined with the early start that the attendance was poor. Most games in the league start at 2.30 p.m. but the London encounter was brought forward to 1.30 p.m. to facilitate the travel arrangements of the visiting team. Also the clocks went forward at 2.00 a.m. so maybe a few people were caught out with the start of summer time.

The game was a lively enough encounter, but Wicklow were in control from early on. Simple errors were being made that had Micko's levels of frustration rising. For example, one of the half-backs was not facing the ball for the kick outs. Kevin instructed Billy Norman to organise the subs to warm-up in threes along the sideline. Brian McGrath is playing very well but is injured on the far sideline following a collision with a London player. He is able to resume but a few minutes later he is in trouble again. His ankle went from under him as he was running and he has to be substituted. At the same time Seánie Furlong suffers a clash of heads in a goalmouth incident, but he is able to continue on. The same player came in for some of Micko's wrath. In another incident, with only the goalkeeper to beat, instead of driving the ball into the net, he tried to place it and the goal opportunity was missed.

At half time the mood was good in the dressing room. Leighton Glynn says: "Keep driving lads. Thirteen scores is not good enough. This game is good practice for us. Track back. Make unselfish runs to the sideline. Keep driving on." Padge McWalter speaks for the first time at halftime, "Winning becomes a habit," he says. Jimmy Whittle points out: "We want three wins back-to-back before Longford. Ignite your brain. We had a good first half."

Micko and the other selectors then come into the changing room. The Maestro begins: "There's one thing above all lads, we're not playing soccer. If you get a goal chance, drive it. Now lads, we don't want any yellow cards. We don't want any talking or giving out to the ref. We have two important games coming up. Take the points. Goals will come. We've scored four fisted points today: that must be a record. We're playing well. Tony, get a bit of fire in your belly. Go at it. You're an outstanding player. Now put a bit of fire into your game. Darren (Hayden), you played last night when you shouldn't."

"They were short," Darren interjects.

Micko responds: "We're short here too." There was one change made for the second half. Darren Hayden was being rested and Cathal McNicholas was going on in his place.

The second half went Wicklow's way. However Dean Odlum was red carded. The referee awarded a free to him but the

London player was slow in releasing the ball. Dean tried to prize it from him and eventually managed to take the free. As he played the ball he was seen by the linesman to kick out at his opponent. The other highlights of this half were the return to the Wicklow jersey of James Stafford and an injury to Damian Power who was replaced by Brian Osborne. The substitute set up Leighton Glynn for Wicklow's twentieth point on the half hour. Close to the final whistle Stafford sent a long ball into Glynn who offloaded it to Seánie Furlong who sent it to the back of the net. Game over.

The mood in the dressing room was upbeat after the game. Micko did not have much to say apart from the big weakness in the Wicklow game of giving the ball away.

TUESDAY 31ST MARCH
Training, Greystones

By the time I got to the Eire Óg GAA Club the session was well under way. The warm-up laps and stretching had finished and there was some sprinting across the pitch. Shorter sprints began with a crouch start. The training ladders were introduced for the first time this year. Players are to take two steps in each space and to change pace as they leave the ladder. The third element of tonight's physical training is the relays. Again the half back line is the line that has to be beaten. Absentees tonight include Tony Hannon who is resting his hamstring, Brian McGrath who came off injured on Sunday (ankle ligaments) and Damian Power who suffered a dead leg in Sunday's match.

Micko addressed the team and referred to Dean Odlum's red card last Sunday. If that had been the championship Wicklow would have been down to 14 men. It would be a total disaster. Dean had let himself and the team down. There is to be no talking to the referee. "Listen, lads, in all my life I have never seen a ref change his mind". Micko had been speaking to the referee of the recent Munster colleges final and no player spoke to the referee. Even when there was a penalty awarded against one team, the players just walked away and said nothing. The penalty was saved.

"On Sunday week we are away to Carlow and the following Sunday we have our final league match at home to Sligo. It is up to us. If clubs ask for county players they are free to train and play as long as it does not clash with county commitments. From now on everyone is to be at training. After all it's you guys who will win the games. Some aspects of our game that will have to be improved are the amount of times we give away the ball. There is also a tendency to fumble with the ball, go to ground and then get up again. When you get the ball your first reaction should be 'Who'll I give it to?' The best scores are got by creating them. For God's sake lads, don't be kicking the ball up into the air. That's a disaster lads. Quick and fast and low. Up in the air and you'll get a fella killed. Basic coaching lads. Get it and in there. Hold it into your chest. You've got to get the basics right. From now on we'll be playing plenty of football – and some training as well. All training will be in Aughrim from next week. You can play with your club as long as it doesn't clash with training."

Jimmy Whittle thanked the panel for their patience with regard to waiting for gear. He assured the panel that the gear will come and come the big day that we they would look well. Philip McGillicuddy had nothing to say except "I'm extremely happy". Next week would be a big week. If Wicklow can beat Kilkenny they will be into the junior final against Kildare.

CHAPTER FOUR

April – What A Shower

WEDNESDAY 1ST APRIL

Against all the odds The Republic of Ireland go to Bari where Italy have never lost a match and come away with a draw. Admittedly the Italians were reduce to ten men in early in the game and then took the lead, but Ireland fought back and equalised in the second half. The debate was who actually scored the equaliser – Robbie Keane was claiming it but so was Noel Hunt. Video clips actually show that it was Keane who got the final touch.

Perhaps what was the most important lesson from this match was that Giovanni Trapattoni was forced to change his usual approach and went out and played attacking football. After Saturday's home draw there was disquiet among the TV pundits about his approach to the game. Tonight's result has forced them to reconsider their opinion of him.

THURSDAY 2ND APRIL
Training, Baltinglass

Glorious sunshine bathed the Garden County and the juniors were to play Kilkenny in Baltinglass this evening, but they conceded the match. Players on the fringe of the senior team should have been playing, but with the match cancelled, there was a large panel for training. Following the warm-up laps and stretching, the ladders were introduced. Micko's encouragement was: "Drive the hell out of it!"

Philip McGillicuddy, Jimmy Whittle and Kevin O'Brien were standing near the finish line, blocking some of the track. Micko's words to the players were: "Any of these in the way knock the down. Drive through them. No pain, no gain lads. That's a well-known fact."

As the session was winding down, all players were called together. Some clubs had matches for the following evening. Players were free to play for their club, but all others must report for training in Roundwood. There would be a night of total football: kicking, kicking, and more kicking – kicking at the goal, kicking across the pitch and free-taking. A player can do all the weights and running alone. In a match what is the number of times you get to kick the ball? Six or seven? That is one aspect of the Wicklow game that must improve – hence the night of total football in Roundwood.

FRIDAY 3RD APRIL
Training in Roundwood
Today the schools got their Easter holidays. I am down in Enniscorthy proof reading the Cumann na mBunscol Náisiúnta annual journal Scoilspórt. I reckon that I should be finished by five or six and will be able to make Roundwood for some of the training. Unfortunately that's not the case – since this is the 125th anniversary of the founding of the GAA, Cumann na mBunscol is including a special commemorative supplement in this year's Scoilspórt called From Cumann na mBunscol to Páirc an Chrócaigh and Beyond.

Each county was asked to submit a short piece on at least one male and one female personality who participated in Cumann na mBunscol events and then went on to represent their county or country. The Garden County submitted pieces on Leighton Glynn. Fionnula Britton and Underdogs stars Caoilfhionn Deeney and Laurie Ahern. I end up leaving the printers at 11pm.

SUNDAY 5TH APRIL
Training in Aughrim

This was another fine morning with plenty of sunshine.

Warm-up laps start off the session and then Billy Norman leads the stretching routine. There are a few sprints back and forward across the pitch. There will be a match of two fifteen minute halves. Again the no hop no solo rule is applied as Micko referees.

I noticed that the portacabin belonging to the Wicklow GAA Supporters Club had not been opened the previous Sunday at the London game. I ask about the club and am told that the Supporters' Club is now defunct. In actual fact it never really got up and running as it was planned. Originally it was to have a dual role: PR and fund-raising. Unfortunately there was no solid structure for the club, and it almost cost as much to run it as it actually made. This is a pity. All you have to do is take a look at what Club Tyrone has done for the GAA in the O'Neill County.

The game is progressing and it is noticeable that the pace has increased compared to the previous few months. The pitch is in great condition and the players are moving the ball swiftly. One forward shoots for a point and sends the ball wide. He lets out an expletive. Micko at once blows for a free and says: "There's no point in f...ing the ball after it's kicked!" While the game is going on an SOS is good humouredly put out for Arthur French who is on the phone. The joke is how can a selector select if he's not at training? One player makes a mistake, and the team administrator slyly remarks in Arthur's earshot: "These are the kinds of things you see when you're at training!"

Micko is encouraging first-time football – quick and fast is his motto. There is a need to get the slowness out of the game. Eleven of the thirty-four on the panel are missing. It is remarked that one particular player does not show up for training when there is a two-week gap between matches – the first week of the gap is usually a tough week and "he has a blister on his foot". Some of the newcomers are doing quite well – Niall Gaffney is one to watch but

Cathal McNicholas is "shallow on confidence". If he makes a mistake it tends to play on his mind and upsets his rhythm for a while. He will need to be coached along gently to learn that when you've made a mistake there is nothing that can undo the error – just try harder not to repeat it. Shane Carthy is also performing well and it is remarked that if he were to do twenty minutes of weights on non-training days that it would make a huge difference to him.

After the match concludes the panel is called together. Micko address them and informs them that there will be training on Tuesday and Thursday here in Aughrim.

He then added: "There is a little man here on my right who has something to do. I have no hand, act or parting it." What he is referring to is Arthur's organisation of a specialist who will meet the team members individually on Good Friday. She is a specialist in bio-energy and will make out a programme for each player.

On Wednesday the junior team will be playing Kildare in Naas. There are a few injury worries – yesterday Ciarán Walsh pulled his hamstring and is undergoing treatment. He will be out of action for a couple of weeks, along with Tony Hannon, Don Jackman and Ciarán Hyland who are also undergoing treatment. The players are encouraged to avail of the ice baths before they shower.

As we are about to depart Aughrim there is a discussion on the jerseys. Arthur and Jimmy want the jersey altered slightly from last year. Both feel that it's important that each year the jersey should be freshened up. It gives a boost to the players, especially the newer members of the panel. Martin is not in favour of changing the jersey – as a parent of three children he sees the expense involved if children want to have the current jersey each year. There are some arguments put forward for and against changing the jersey. Despite common opinion it is said that the Dublin jersey is not the biggest selling jersey in the country. Much to everyone's surprise we are told that Offaly is the biggest seller of jerseys – apparently because of the tricolour it is used my many supporters of the various international sides. There is also the debate about the style of jersey – should it be a traditional jersey or one of the increasingly popular skin-tight ones? The advantage of the skin-tight jersey is that it is much more difficult for an opponent to grab hold of and pull. The next discussion concerns the water that is supplied to the team. Is it going to be River Rock or Kerry Spring? Last year it was Kerry Spring and the understanding was that it was to be the same this year. However River Rock is being supplied. Arthur is of the opinion that the water from the Kingdom is far superior to that of River Rock. He feels that we are not getting it because it is dearer and that the County Board are trying to cut costs. Martin is compared to an egg-timer – all issues from the panel come through him to the County Board. He will raise the issue of the water at the next meeting. Micko, through his contacts in his native county, will be able to source Kerry Spring at cost. The final gripe of the day is the absence of three minor players from Blessington who have had to pull out of the county panel – apparently there was no one available to bring them to training. Three other Blessington players have pulled out of the junior panel. The parting comment at this news is that it must be something in the water in Blessington.

TUESDAY 7TH APRIL
Training in Aughrim
Today was the day of the Supplementary Budget. After starting off fine and sunny the rain came in the mid afternoon and continued well into the night. It is also quite windy. Training begins with some warm-up laps, followed by stretching and sprints across the pitch. There is the usual practice match of yellows against reds. The pitch is quite solid but the wet conditions make it slippy. Apart from Micko who is in the middle of the pitch refereeing the rest of the back-room seek shelter in the dug-out. Conditions are most unpleasant.

This is the first night of evening training in Aughrim – the sign that the championship is just around the corner. It was more like a wintery afternoon in November than a spring evening. After the match there is a session with the ladders followed by some sprints up and down the pitch. Kevin O'Brien urges everyone to drive with their arms as they are going through the ladders. It is noticeable that those who have trained for soccer are much more fluent with this apparatus. Everyone is thankful when the session comes to an end. A few of the players opt for the ice bath before the hot shower. Definitely not for the faint-hearted!

HOLY THURSDAY 9TH APRIL
Training in Aughrim

It is a pleasant evening and there are thirty players at training. (The junior team lost to Kildare on a score line of 0-13 to 1-8.) Training consists of a practice match. At the end of the session the squad is called together and the arrangements for Sunday's match are explained. There will not be a bus for this game in Carlow. In these recessionary times it does not make sense to hire a bus for a journey that will take less than an hour. Micko tells the players of the importance of the match against Carlow. Wicklow beat them already in the first round of the O'Byrne Cup in January, but since then Luke Dempsey has been building a team that is capable of putting it up to The Garden County. Complacency is the big enemy. Division three football is within our grasp. A win against Carlow on Easter Sunday and the following Sunday there is home match against Sligo.

Arthur addresses the players and talks of the dedication of Micko. Micko left Waterville this afternoon and drove straight to Aughrim. He had a meal in Lawless' Hotel and then took charge of training. He is now going to have a quick cup of tea and will then drive back to Waterville. That is a round trip of 500 miles. On top of that, Micko is 72 years of age. That is dedication and leadership. That's they sort of commitment that Wicklow needs. That's the

Ciarán Hyland shows the selectors how to do chin-ups

Arthur French, Martin Coleman and Micko leaving The Glenview Hotel ahead of the O'Byrne Cup challenge against the Dubs

The Wicklow team about to take on the Dubs in Parnell Park. Left: Seánie Furlong cannot believe that he has been sent off

Wicklow supporters in Casement Park in Belfast for the 2009 league opening round against Antrim

Micko poses with a young supporter after a training session

On a visit to St. Coman's Hospital Rathdrum during the Rose of Avondale Festival

Jimmy Whittle in action

Noel Molloy, Martin Coleman, Pat Kelly, Peter Keogh (RIP) and Premnath Margabaandan

Above: Noel Molloy working his magic

Right: Spineologist Pat Kelly working on Arthur French as Michael Murphy looks on

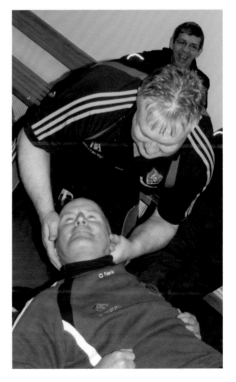

The President fears no one – Peter Keogh telling Dublin midfielder Ciarán Whelan a thing or two!

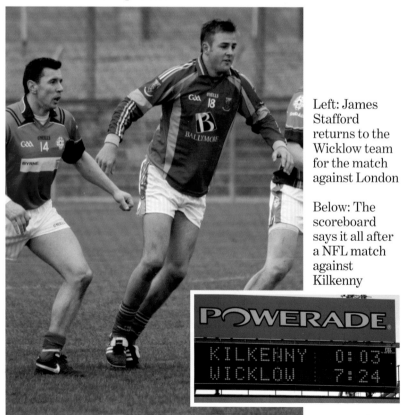

Left: James Stafford returns to the Wicklow team for the match against London

Below: The scoreboard says it all after a NFL match against Kilkenny

A dejected Micko ponders on what might have been following the defeat to Leitrim

Brendan Hayden and Micko meet up in Dr. Cullen Park fifty years after playing against each other

Martin Coleman. Philip McGillicuddy, Arthur French and Martin Lott shelter from the rain during the first evening training session of the season in Aughrim

Thomas Walsh lining out for the first time in 2009 for Wicklow

Micko, Peter Keogh, Des Burton and Bríd Owens, Principal of Sacred Heart NS Aughrim with Peter's great grandchildren during the 125 Schools Day

Stephen Fanning enjoying a post-training ice bath

Martin Coleman explaining to Kevin O'Brien the importance of the Liam MacCarthy trophy

Philip McGillycuddy shows his delight to an incredulous Padge McWalter after the final whistle in the victory over Longford

Arthur French demonstrates how to kick a placed ball watched from left to right by Cathal McNicholas, James Stafford, Alan Byrne, Seánie Furlong and Rory Nolan

sort of commitment that Wicklow never had. There is to be no player playing club football until further notice.

After the teams depart the pitch, Paul Earls, who is home on holiday from his studies in the UK, stays out and practises his free-taking. Philip McGillicuddy has a DVD which features some of the game against Leitrim. He focuses in some of the better scores, the scores when we played direct football.

GOOD FRIDAY 10TH APRIL
Lawless Hotel, Aughrim

The players have been asked to meet with Hazel Devine, a bio-energy expert. Hazel has a room in Lawless Hotel where she has individual consultations with each of the players. Each consultation lasts for about 30 minutes, and every man who comes out simply says that it was awesome. Without trying to pry too much, all I can get out of any of the players is that she asks a few questions and if you do no answer honestly she will tell you so and enlighten you as to what is the honest answer. I am intrigued and pick up a flyer. It reads:

I was born with a natural ability to see what is going on in people's lives. I can look at the past, present and future to help people with what is going on in their life at present. I do not interfere with a person's future because each person creates their own future. If I need to guide them I will. I work with energy and I look at people's health. When a person comes to me with a symptom I go back into their life to find out what caused them to develop the symptom in the first place. While I was aware from a very young age that I had this ability, I only started to fully come into it, in later years while going through my own health difficulties. I teach classes also to show people how to look at their own lives and to learn how to take back their control, trust and belief in themselves to bring complete balance in their lives.

Areas that she deals with include physical health, thoughts and emotions. Arthur was responsible for bringing Hazel to meet the players in order to increase their levels of energy. He believes in alternative medical practices and he had read in Michael Flatley's biography that the dancer had experienced some serious health problems. Flatley attended a Mayo based practitioner of bio energy, Tom Griffin, who had been able to heal the dancer. Arthur made contact with Tom who recommended Hazel. Hazel, according to Griffin, is the best practitioner of bio energy in the world. It had been difficult to get Hazel to come to Wicklow as she had a very full diary, but Good Friday was the day that was agreed. Paddy Dalton, Jacko Dalton were just two of the players who had had their consultation while I was there and both were positive about what they had heard from Hazel.

Arthur told me when it became known that he and Micko were coming to Wicklow that the common opinion was that they were mad. There was the theory that the mountains divided the county and that Wicklow was home to a divided people with plenty of fighting among themselves, and of course the notorious incident of the ref in the boot. Micko's response to all of this was: "We like a little challenge." Under Micko the training regime is relaxed and light-hearted. Hugh Kenny during his time as manager was unfortunate not to gain promotion from division four and had a few narrow defeats in the championship. It must also be remembered that Hugh Kenny was one of, if not the youngest inter county managers at the time. Apparently there was a poor atmosphere in the Wicklow camp before Hugh.

EASTER SUNDAY 12TH APRIL
National Football League Division Four, Round Six,
Dr. Cullen Park, Carlow
Carlow 2-15 Wicklow 3-7
As I am travelling to Donegal later today to represent Cumann na mBunscol Náisiúnta at the trade fair at the Irish National

Teachers' Organisation Annual Congress I decide to go straight to Dr. Cullen Park rather than meet in Baltinglass. I arrive at the ground a few minutes before any of the Wicklow squad. The last time I was in Dr. Cullen Park was in June when Laois defeated Wicklow in the Leinster championship. Wicklow should have won that game. They stood back from Laois and gave them too much respect. By the time that Wicklow began to believe in themselves they had let the gap grow too wide. Despite a sterling performance in the second half and a rasping shot from James Stafford that hit off the crossbar at a vital stage of the game, Laois held on to win. Exit Wicklow from the 2008 championship and no qualifier route for division four teams. In fact, the more I think of it, I have never been to a game at the Carlow venue that Wicklow won.

Micko addresses the team before the throw-in. In an earlier throw-in Waterford are at home to Sligo. Sligo are leading in Markievicz Park. If Sligo can defeat Waterford Wicklow are back in with a chance of promotion to division three … provided they can beat Carlow today. "Right lads, you know the team. Jacko and James Stafford are at midfield. Don Jackman is on the forty with Paul Earls. I don't need to tell you the importance of today's game. We don't get involved with the ref. This guy is good (John Bannon). If you start nagging he'll turn against you and the team. There will be decisions that go against you. Your first reaction should always be 'Where's my man?' Jacko, let it go quickly. Look lads, we want total commitment. One hour and 10 minutes of football. This is a game we must win."

Before the game, as Micko is making his way to the dug out, he meets a man of his own vintage. This man is Brendan Hayden, who 53 years ago played for Carlow against Micko and Kerry. Brendan played with Carlow for many years and also represented Leinster on numerous occasions. A newcomer to the Wicklow back room is physiotherapist Prem, (Premnath Margabandan), who hails from India and who will be assisting Noel with treating the players.

Wicklow get off to the perfect start with a Paul Earls goal in the first minute. Wicklow get a second goal during the first half and it's looking good. Word filters through that Sligo won by three points. Promotion from division four is now in our own hands.

At half time Jimmy rallies the troops. "That was top class reaction to the ref. Leighton you have been exemplary."

Leighton Glynn: "Playing the way we did in the first 20 minutes we would beat anyone. Then we went back to the shit carrying that got us nowhere. They got seven of their nine scores from frees. They only got two scores from play. We've got to up our work rate."

The manager comes into the changing room and it is obvious that he is agitated.

"Look lads, that's crazy stuff. We gave them six frees and they got six points. Leighton, Rory for God's sake don't be over attacking. Keep tight. Jacko, we need a real big effort from you. Midfielders, you must contest the kick outs. Half forwards and half backs you must watch the breaks. The big men will get it. Darragh O'Sullivan you hopped the ball in front of the goal and you lost it. You should have taken your point. Now lads, we want a big effort this half. And for God's sake stop the fouling! You're pulling out of tackles. What are you scared of? Get out there and die for Wicklow."

The second half does not go according to plan. Don Jackman comes off with a hamstring injury and John McGrath suffers a broken collar bone. Wicklow are awarded a penalty and the offender is red carded. Paul Earls takes the penalty and misses. Seánie Furlong comes off with an ankle injury – it later transpires that he did not get it strapped up before the game. Seánie knows that he should have – valuable lesson for the future.

In what many see as a very peculiar decision, Billy Norman, the reserve goalkeeper is put on as full forward. The thinking is that Billy is a very big man and if the ball can be sent into him he'll cause panic in the Carlow defence. This does not work and there is much criticism of the management among the supporters after the game. One opinion expressed is why should a player train for months as a forward and when there is a substitution to be made to see the reserve goalkeeper going on? Has Dwyer lost the plot? Are the criticisms of his training methods justified? Surely they should be playing football in training and not doing laps? Is there disquiet in the camp? Is he just going through the motions?

In the changing room after the game Micko tries to rally the troops. "Right lads, I don't have to tell you how bad you were. Real training begins on Tuesday. Weddings and twenty-firsts – all that is over. We'll have a hard training session on Tuesday. That was a terrible display and they're not even a good Carlow team. Our fitness is not near where it should be. Everyone at training on Tuesday. We don't want fellas feigning injury. We'll start on Tuesday and take it from there. This was only the league. May 24 is the big one but we're far from where we need to be."

MONDAY 13TH APRIL
INTO Congress, Letterkenny

I arrive at the Hotel Letterkenny and begin to set up the stand. It is a very wet morning. Two Kilkenny delegates arrive as I am setting up the stand and hand me a black plastic bag. Inside is the Liam McCarthy Cup. I am responsible for it until Friday when I will deliver it to the Round Towers GAA Club in Clondalkin where it will be on display at a juvenile medal presentation ceremony. There is much interest in the Liam McCarthy and I tell visitors to the stand to come again tomorrow as Sam Maguire is due to attend. I am joined, for some time at the stand by the secretary of Cumann na mBunscol Náisiúnta Paul Duggan and the Primary Schools Co-ordinator from Croke Park Micheál Martin. Joining me for the remainder of the day are Selina O'Regan from the GAA Museum and Annmarie Smith from the GAA Oral History Project. Both girls will stay helping at the stand until Congress closes on Wednesday.

TUESDAY 14TH APRIL
INTO Congress, Letterkenny

Tuesday night means training and Micko promised that it would be a heavy session. Unfortunately I will not be able to attend. By mid-morning there is a great commotion. Cuthbert Donnelly, guardian of Sam Maguire, arrives from Tyrone with the famous piece of silverware. At a request from Declan Kelleher, President of the Irish National Teachers' Organisation, both the Sam Maguire and Liam MacCarthy cups are brought to the conference hall where there is a rousing reception for them. Declan, a Clareman, makes an issue of rubbing Liam.

WEDNESDAY 15TH APRIL

It is reported that Thomas Walsh has pledged his future to Wicklow for the rest of the year after making his seasonal return to training last night. The highly-rated midfielder has been convinced to stay with the Garden County, to whom he controversially transferred from Carlow two years ago, although Wicklow county board chairman Andy O'Brien has strongly denied reports that manager Mick O'Dwyer made a visit to the player in an effort to encourage him back into the squad.

Rumours have been rife in Carlow that O'Dwyer was seen at the Walsh home in Fenagh trying to bring him back into the fold. But O'Brien insisted: "There was no way Mick O'Dwyer was at Thomas Walsh's house." Carlow manager Luke Dempsey was hopeful that Walsh would return to play with his native county in this year's championship after playing rugby with Tullow for the winter, but it now appears that he has failed in his quest to lure back to former Leinster player, who qualifies to play for Wicklow due to the fact that he lives in the county and plays his club football with Bray Emmets.

"Walsh Returns to Garden Party"

Frank Roche reports in The Evening Herald that Thomas Walsh had made a dramatic eve-of-championship return to the Wicklow football panel – much to the chagrin of his native Carlow. Question marks have also been raised about Walsh's eligibility to play for his adopted county, following several reports in recent months that he was back living in Carlow, but the Wicklow county board understands that the big midfielder is still resident at his Wicklow address. Wicklow sources have confirmed that Walsh resumed training for the first time last night with Mick O'Dwyer's panel. He hasn't played any National League football this spring, playing rugby with Tullow RFC instead, and it was widely felt that he would not play any inter-county football this year.

New Carlow boss Luke Dempsey had spent a number of months courting Walsh, initially confident that he would rejoin Carlow, only to give up the chase last March. When told this morning of the latest development in this long-running saga, Carlow chairman Pat Deering expressed his personal disappointment with the player's decision. It was Deering's stated belief that the Fenagh native has been back living at his parent's home in Carlow.

But when asked about the residency issue, Wicklow secretary Michael Murphy said it was his understanding that he was still resident at the Wicklow address that was given when he moved to the county. He also understood that Walsh had "indicated to his club, Bray Emmets, that he would be playing with them this year."

Under GAA rules, he must remain resident in Wicklow and be a member of a local club if he's to qualify for his adopted county. Murphy confirmed that they will clarify the residency issue, adding: "Obviously we won't put ourselves in a position that someone can come along and object that he wasn't eligible to play for us."

The Wicklow secretary said it was "certainly news to me" when told that Walsh had trained with the county last night.

"We tried at the start of the year to see would he come over to us at the start of the league, and he indicated that he was playing rugby at the time," Murphy added. "Since that, I haven't heard anything over the last two weeks to indicate that he was coming back ... I didn't think, from all the rumours going around, that he was going to play football at all this year.

"Then the people in Bray were saying they had been talking to him and, at the start of the year, he indicated he would be playing (with them)."

It's safe to assume that Dempsey won't be overly enamoured of Walsh's Wicklow comeback. Last March, he accepted that he and his brother Patrick would not be returning to the Carlow panel, saying: "At this stage all I can say is that I utterly disappointed with them."

THURSDAY 14TH APRIL
Training in Aughrim

It is a very wet evening in Aughrim. Tonight Kevin O'Brien is refereeing. At the end of training Micko addresses the players: "Now look lads, the 24th of May is only five weeks away from Sunday. It's do or die from now on. Discipline has to be our number one. Two or three of you are sneaking off and playing for your clubs. From now on we want total commitment." Martin Coleman has a slip of paper for everyone with the dates and venues for every training session up to the Longford match. There will be eighteen more sessions before the opening round of the championship. Micko continues, "You know yourselves lads, the first of the dates is Saturday. Be here for half one. You know exactly what you have to do. This Sunday will be your last games for your clubs. We don't want anyone playing a game this Friday night. The first six points Carlow got were from frees because of fouls with the arms. Tackle the ball not the man. Leave the player on the ground. Stand around him and we'll get a free. If we get a free, look and kick - we're delaying looking for a kicker. The man who's fouled should take the free. Jesus lads, you're inter county players. You're all capable of taking a quick free. Backs, we want you to play more defensively. These are the basic little things. Put resin on your hands. The ball is slipping. Get the ball into your chest. In here and then get rid of it. Jesus, it's all about determination. We need to put a bit of fire into our game."

Upstairs in the complex the players have their post match meal. I am still in possession of the Liam MacCarthy so I bring it up and place it on the table before the players arrive upstairs. The joke when they start arriving is that they are wondering what this wine cooler is. Martin Coleman, a hurling fan, is in his element explaining to all and sundry that this is a real trophy. Micko looks at the cup and we all know that he believes that there is really only one cup ... Some of the players take turns holding it and there are photographs taken of them. Some are secretly thinking that wouldn't it be fantastic if this were the Sam Maguire and if it were residing in Wicklow for the next year ....

SATURDAY 18TH APRIL
Sligo 0-11 Wicklow 0-10

In advance today was dubbed Super Saturday. The weather is perfect for such a day – bright and sunny and there is even a little bit of warmth. It is a double header in Aughrim: the minors, of whom much is expected, are playing Kildare in the championship. The seniors, if they had beaten Carlow last Sunday, would have been going head-to-head with Sligo for promotion to division three. Super Saturday will not be so super after all – our chances of promotion ended on Easter Sunday in Dr. Cullen Park. The minors are destroyed by Kildare on a score line of 4-19 to 0-5. Not a good start to Super Saturday.

I sense the mood is not good amongst the selectors. In Cork at the GAA Congress the new rules motion was defeated by eight votes. A two-thirds majority would have been needed, and that was almost achieved. Padge McWalter and Rory Nolan have stomach bugs and are not fit to play. John McGrath's collar bone is broken and he will be out of action for six weeks at least. Micko speaks quietly to John and tries to console him. He advises the injured player to continue to attend training and receive treatment. Our new physiotherapist, Prem, is asked his opinion of Gaelic football and he replies: "It is a very challenging game. It is very tough."

Cathal McNicholas, a recruit from the U-21s has been drafted into the panel, but during the warm-up he feels a twinge in his hamstring. At ten past two the team re-enters the dressing room and the jerseys are given out. There is the usual applause as each player receives the county jersey. Micko addresses the panel: "Now lads, get up. We're using some new fellas today. It's your chance to make an impression. We want to give everyone a fair crack of the whip. Play with fire and power. Defenders we want you play tight and close to your man. Half backs we don't want you to be doing too much attacking. Midfielders play it in quick and fast. We want you to be more defensive today."

Tony Hannon is disappointed that he is not in the panel for today. Arthur explains to him that they are not risking him today as there is nothing to be gained from today's match. Tony accepts this.

The game starts and it is one of those frustrating matches where nothing seems to be going right. After twenty minutes full back Damian Power is red carded. That just sums up the first half – the full back was not having his best game in the number three jersey.

At half time Micko comes into the dressing room and has change on his mind: "Lads we're going to make a few changes. Jesus lads, there's no point in going up for the ball with one hand hoping. Dean, go and kill some fella! Cathal McNicholas, have you got fire in your belly? Shane Carthy, for God's sake don't be kicking it into the goalie. Backs are playing well. Dean Odlum, you're the fittest man on the pitch. Go to midfield and be the third midfielder. Paul

Earls you'll have lots of room now. Darragh O'Sullivan, put a bit of fire in your belly. Why are you training? We have to fight and harass. There's no point in standing and looking at it. Full backs and half backs are playing well. Jacko? Let it go sooner..."

The second half is close with little separating the teams. Towards the end of the second half the linesman warns the Wicklow bench that the subs will be put into the stand if they do not moderate their language. Decisions are going against Wicklow and it seems that it is going to be another one of those frustrating afternoons.

A peculiarity of Aughrim: the scoreboard faces the sun and apparently the sun can cause problems with it. The score will change automatically and occasionally the operator cannot get the correct score back. With very little time to go the scoreboard reads 0-11 to 0-9 in favour of Sligo when it should be 0-11 to 0-10. With time almost up Leighton Glynn found himself going forward. The only chance Wicklow had was to try and get the goal. A point would be no good at this late stage. Leighton drove in one of his trademark shots, but unfortunately it was parried and cleared away. Full time whistle: Sligo win.It later transpired that the scoreboard was wrong and that Leighton thought that we were two points behind and therefore he had no choice but to go for goal. Had he known the real score he would have tapped it over for a point and Wicklow would have ended up with a share of the spoils.

County board chairman Andy O'Brien said that he was fed up with excuses. Today it was the scoreboard – a bad end to a bad day. The league ended today and Wicklow are still in division four. But at least there is some hope and consolation in what Micko says that his focus at all times has been on the championship and that had we got promotion it would have been a bonus.

In the dressing room Micko tells the players that the real training will start on Monday. There will be a busy week. Our discipline was good today and we did give a good display. The new players performed well today and are in the running for places on the championship team. Players will be allowed to play for the clubs tomorrow should they wish to do so.

The curtain has come down on the 2009 national league. The record will show that Wicklow finished mid table in fifth place ahead of Clare, Carlow, London and Kilkenny. Antrim and Sligo were promoted and next were Leitrim and Waterford. Wicklow won three, lost three and drew two, amassing one hundred and fifty-three points and conceding one hundred and two. Had the Sligo match ended in a draw The Garden County would have finished in fourth place ahead of Waterford on scoring difference.

MONDAY 20TH APRIL
Training in Aughrim

It is a beautiful day in Wicklow and tonight the panel is split into two groups. Both sets of players are doing various exercises. There are lots of sprints over various distances: to the 13, 20 and 45 metre lines. There are some longer sprints from the centre of the pitch around the goals and back to the middle of the field. Tonight there are also ball drills which entail plenty of passing and running. There are only five weeks to go until the championship opener but the injury list is growing. Damian Power is suffering from a groin injury and this season he has been plagued with injury. The position of full-back is now causing concern.

At the end of the session Micko calls the panel together and tells them about how Maurice Fitzgerald and Dara Ó Sé would each do eight laps of the pitch every night. Micko says that there will be three weeks of training followed by two weeks of winding down. Tomorrow we will play football. If players cannot play tomorrow the manager reckons that they will not be able to play on 24th May. Over the post-training meal, Micko expresses his annoyance that there is no minor league structure in Wicklow. Blessington minors play in the Dublin league while the Baltinglass U-18s play in Kildare.

TUESDAY 21ST APRIL
Training in Aughrim

The big news is that Thomas Walsh is back. After months of speculation, Walshie has resumed training with Wicklow. Along with James Stafford, the county now has a midfield pairing that is as good as, if not better than, any partnership in the country. There is a fifteen-a-side match tonight that is played with more urgency than I have seen before.

Micko asks the players why they persist in kicking the ball into the corners. Use the direct route, he encourages. Attack through the middle. Following the game there are eight laps to be run. Some players really struggle with this aspect of training. As they are recovering from the laps Micko informs them that there will be a challenge match against Roscommon in Ballymore Eustace on Friday night. Everyone should be there and all fringe players will get a chance. He tells them that his training methods have been questioned with people saying that they are antiquated. He tells the players that Dara Ó Sé would say that he was only ready to win an All Ireland when he was near the front at the end of the eight lap run.

Later, over the meal the usual banter gets into full swing. Martin Coleman is wondering what's happening in Desperate Housewives on television and Kevin O'Brien responds: "Look Martin, we're trying to win a Leinster here and you're wondering what's going on in Desperate Housewives?" Kevin tells me that none of the panel is married, and the way things are going that no one else might be either at the end of this campaign.

FRIDAY 24TH APRIL
Challenge match in Ballymore Eustace
Roscommon 1-12 Wicklow 2-8

Today was designated GAA 125 Schools Day to mark the founding of the association. School were encouraged to allow the children to wear their favourite GAA jersey, to have some GAA-related activities and to try to get some well known personality to visit the school. As PRO of Wicklow Cumann na mBunscol I was honoured to drive Micko and Peter Keogh to eight different schools during the day and to talk to the children. In fact at some of the venues pupils from neighbouring schools were able to come along too. It is estimated that over one thousand children got to listen to Micko on this day as he spoke to them about the importance of physical exercise, the enjoyment and friendship that sport brings and the dangers of smoking and overindulging in alcohol.

The day began at 9.10 with a visit to St. Joseph's NS in Baltinglass. The school was decorated in the green and white of the local club and the blue and yellow of Wicklow. Members of the Baltinglass All Ireland Club winning side were also present. (Principal of the school is Tom Hannifin, a Kerry man who introduced many of the Baltinglass team to Gaelic football.) Each pupil was also asked to bring in some GAA artefact in honour of the day. Kevin O'Brien's daughters managed to persuade their dad to let them bring in his All Star award.

The next stop was Talbotstown NS, a small rural school with less than a hundred pupils. Peter Keogh often takes the children from this school training and when the party arrived at the school, the entire school population was at the front of the school to welcome Micko. Peter was thrilled to show off the Kiltegan 2008 county champion's calendar to Micko. Attending the school was a five year old nephew of Seánie Furlong who was wearing the colours of his famous uncle's club.

From there it was on to The Sacred Heart School in Aughrim where grandchildren of Peter Keogh's are students. There was a large turn out from the local community and one of the teachers made sure that the Kerry maestro saw her Cork jersey. From there it was on to the Gaelscoil in Arklow. There is actually no school building as such – it's a collection of prefabs on the grounds of the local soccer club. It says a lot about the priorities of the nation's government. Two of the staff of the Gaelscoil are Kerrymen and

Dublin senior footballer and winner of the a Club All Ireland with Kilmacud Crokes this year, Darren Magee, is employed by the local AGB GAA Club to coach in the local schools. Pupils from other schools in Arklow were also in attendance and there was plenty of time for posing for photographs and for signing jerseys. St. Patrick's BNS in Wicklow Town was the next stop and following his address to the pupils Micko and Peter had a welcome cup of tea.

From there it was up to the mountains of Glendalough where the pupils from Scoil Chaoimhín Naofa were joined by their neighbours from Roundwood. Back down the hills again to Newtown where the local community was out in force in the national school. Introducing Micko in Newtown was local teacher, Jim O'Riordan, who is also chairperson of Cumann na mBunscol Cill Mhantáin. Jim was wearing his red People's Republic of Cork T-Shirt which sports pictures of Ché Guvera, Fidel Castro, Lenin and Michael Collins. One of the local community had an original match programme from the 1965 Galway v Kerry All Ireland final in which Micko played. An autograph was a must.

The eighth and final stop was in Kilcoole where the principal of the boys' school, Joanne MacDonagh is a daughter of the late, great Galway and Connacht star Mattie MacDonagh, who played against Micko in that 1965 final. Girls from the convent joined the boys for this the last visit of the day. It was then time to return to Baltinglass and to have something to eat. Soon it would be time to head to Ballymore Eustace for the Roscommon game.

Today was also the day of the wedding of Aisling O'Brien, daughter of county chairman Andy O'Brien. Both Martin Coleman and Jimmy Whittle are at the wedding, so it is up to the county administrator to have all the paperwork in order. Even though it is just a challenge match it is vital that all the correct boxes are ticked. This will be Thomas Walsh's first match for Wicklow since last year's Tommy Murphy Cup final. After the debacle that preceded his transfer to Wicklow two years ago, the last thing that Wicklow needs is a repeat of the same.

The game is entertaining enough, even though both teams are far from championship standard. Roscommon are going to Wexford following the game for a weekend training camp. The game is played in a good spirit with Wicklow's premier midfield pairing playing together for the first time in almost a year. The pitch is rather narrow, a condition that does not suit the Wicklow style of play, but what Micko is looking for is the team to play nice football, fast and quick and direct. At half time the score is 1-8 to 1-4 in favour of Roscommon. The passing from Wicklow is quite poor. The Roscommon free taker is taking at least 25 seconds to kick each free. Arthur French knows this because he has timed him. When the Roscommon man prepares to take his next free Arthur shouts out, "In your own time!" much to the amusement of everyone within earshot. At the final whistle darkness is falling and although Wicklow double their scoring tally in the second half the Connacht men manage to maintain their four point advantage. Bray's Paul Cunningham makes his senior inter-county debut in this game and shows up well.

During the post match meal both teams are sharing the one dining room. There is good rapport between the two sides and Micko and the Roscommon manager, Fergal O'Donnell, spend some time talking to each other. (There is yet another Wicklow connection today – Fergal O'Donnell's brother, Shane, is Principal Teacher in St. Joseph's NS Glenealy.)

Kevin O'Brien tells me that he was asked to visit Crossbridge School today as part of the GAA 125 schools Day. He did so and there were the colours from the home school, Knockananna, Tinahely and Wicklow adorning the hall. Kevin was treated to a rendition of An Ode to Micko a song that the pupils and their teachers composed for the occasion. Elsewhere Baltinglass brothers and Wicklow panellists, Rory and Alan Nolan visited Grangecon NS where they had hoped to do some coaching with the children, but unfortunately the weather was not conducive to this.

SATURDAY 25TH APRIL
Training in Aughrim

By the time training began at 11 o'clock the rain had stopped and the weather had begun to brighten up. Today was the day of the Wicklow Coaching Conference in Roundwood. Micko was present for the opening session.

Now it was time for the practical - following the usual warm up routine there was a series of sprints back and forth across the pitch. Today Kevin was calling out a player's name if he were pulling up before the finish line. "Sloppy in training, sloppy in a match" is his motto. There is a short practice match followed by a passing drill involving sets of three players.

There were calls to increase the pace of this drill to which the players responded positively. At the end of the session Micko reminds the players that they are not to play any club matches before the Longford game for fear of picking up an injury. Wicklow, of all teams, cannot afford to have any injuries. In the minor championship Wicklow defeated Carlow on a score line of 2-12 to 1-8.

The rehabilitation of the minor team following the heavy defeat at the hands of Kildare has begun. (A connection between the minor teams of Wicklow and Carlow: Noel Molloy's son is on the Carlow team.) This afternoon in Longford, Sligo defeat Antrim in the league final by two points (1-12 to 1-10). Later Tipperary defeat Down 0-18 to 1-14 to be crowned division three champions. Last year Tipperary edged out Wicklow to gain promotion to Division 3. This year they gain promotion to division two. Wicklow cannot be far behind.

SUNDAY 26TH APRIL

Kerry beat Derry 1-15 to 0-15 in Croke Park to take their nineteenth league title. Of those nineteen, Micko managed eight of the teams. Earlier on at the same venue Cork defeat Monaghan 1-14 to 0-12 to take the Division Two title.

MONDAY 27TH APRIL
Training in Aughrim

This evening it is quite pleasant. There is a 15-a-side practice match during which soloing is allowed. I learn that Arthur French was an usher at the wedding of the American ambassador's daughter recently. As usual there is plenty to be said about the circles in which Arthur moves.

After the match Micko tells the players that they made some great interceptions against Roscommon on Friday last. The game was played largely between the two 21s, but we made some basic errors that caused a break down in our play. He tells the players that there were some harsh calls, for example, for dubious pick ups. He reminds them that these are basic errors and could cost us if they happened in the last five minutes of an important clash. He advises players who are in possession of the ball to be careful about being caught out near the end line. "You should always be thinking who can I give it to?' Don't be afraid to play it back out the field. And for God's sake lads, don't be blinking or going for the ball with your eyes shut. You'll lose it." He then comments on Sligo's and Tipperary's league victories and tells them: "You're up there with the best."

TUESDAY 28TH APRIL
Training in Aughrim

Today was Wicklow race Day in Punchestown. Micko and Arthur were present during the afternoon. Arthur was called upon to auction a race and earned €4,250 for the county board, a not insubstantial sum in these recessionary times. Micheál Ó Muirtheachaigh interviewed Peter Keogh. The interview came round to the 1954 Leinster championship match between Meath and Wicklow which the Royals won by one point. Peter named the entire Wicklow team and informed Micheál that the Royals went on to win the All Ireland that year.

Training began as usual and then two small games were

played across the pitch with the emphasis on fist passing. Later there is a fifteen-a-side match on the full pitch. As usual Micko calls the players together at the end of the session. He tells them that there are some basic needs in their play. "When going forward there could be nine or ten of your own team behind you. Why keep going forward and run into trouble? If there is a free man behind you, use him." He reminds them that for every point they score the opposition has to score two to win. He says he is heartened to see most players beginning to play intelligent football. Breaking down attacks is improving and there are only twenty-six days to the Longford game. "We're looking good."

THURSDAY 30TH APRIL
Training in Aughrim
Tonight the hurdles are in use. The hurdles which were designed by Jimmy Whittle are very effective. There is a good atmosphere among the panel and soon it is time for the practice match. It is reds against yellows and the no hop, no solo rule is applied at first. As usual Micko is refereeing. Passing tonight is very sloppy. There is too much attacking and not enough defending. Since there are only twenty-four participating in the match it is twelve-a-side. The pitch has been shortened to accommodate the smaller number on each team.

Arlene attends training tonight. Arlene is Arthur's daughter and she has an interest, like Arthur in alternative therapies. After training the players are weighed and a comparison is made with the last time she weighed them. Some players have gained weight - some has been as a result of the gym work, but unfortunately other players have gained weight for the wrong reasons.

None has gained an excessive amount of weight and one or two of the lads are told that they could do with gaining a little more. There are some players who have lost weight.

And so the end of April has drawn in upon us. Four months since this whole project began. The first round of the Leinster Championship is just twenty-four days away.

CHAPTER FIVE

Selectors And The French Connection

ARTHUR FRENCH

Arthur French is a 60 plus year old successful businessman who runs an auctioneering firm in Leixlip. Originally from near Claremorris in Mayo, he is also a member of the board of Knock Airport. Arthur played minor, U-21 and senior for his native county. In the early seventies he won a senior football championship with Claremorris. He moved to Dublin shortly afterwards where he worked as a sales representative for GWI, a Sligo-based company. Arthur feels that his involvement in football certainly helped to secure his employment.

He eventually settled in Kildare and played football with Leixlip and Kildare. Arthur is not the tallest of men, but he filled the role of corner forward very well. He was also quite an expert free taker. Indeed, most nights at training Arthur kicks dozens of placed balls for about 20 minutes or more. Often Micko would call the panel together to watch Arthur take a free. He seldom missed anything from inside 40 metres.

Arthur managed the Leixlip team for some time, but he never won a senior championship with them. On the occasions the club made it as far as the county semi-final, they lost to both Clane and Johnstown Bridge. He was instrumental in bringing Kerry's Jack O'Shea to the Leixlip club. Arthur also won two All Ireland medals with the Kildare over-40s team.

Arthur told me Micko and he have been friends for many years. In their younger days Arthur and his family would often holiday in Waterville where he and Micko enjoyed golf and football. Over the years the two men consolidated their friendship. I asked Arthur how he and Micko ended up running the Wicklow senior football team. He told me that it is well documented in Martin Breheny's biography of Micko, Blessed and Obsessed. Briefly, Arthur met the Fine Gael TD Billy Timmons at a funeral in Kilcock in 2006. Billy had been a member of the Baltinglass team that won the club championship in 1990. The Wicklow man asked Arthur if there would be any chance that the Waterville Maestro would manage Wicklow, and as they say: "The rest is history."

When asked why they came to Wicklow, Arthur said that managing the Garden County was the greatest challenge ever for Micko. The cynics and knockers maintain that any manager could have achieved what Micko had achieved in Kerry with the pool of talent at his disposal. Wicklow were ranked 31st in the national footballing stakes.

There was a similar introduction for Micko to Kildare. When he joined the Lilywhites in the early 1990s they were at an all-time low ... Kilkenny had beaten them in the O'Byrne Cup. In Laois there was a 57-year barren spell without a Leinster title. However both Kildare and Laois had plenty of talent. In his time with Kildare, Micko won two Leinster titles and guided them to an All Ireland final appearance in 1998. He managed Laois when they won their first Leinster title in 57 years in 2003.

To secure Micko, it was necessary to have certain structures in place, not least of which was a significant sponsor. Seán Mulryan of Ballymore properties had an involvement with Wicklow over the years. Originally from Roscommon, the Mulryans are members of the Hollywood Club. In 2006 the construction industry was flying. Arthur's philosophy is: "If it's right I'll go with it." He follows what he believes and his instinct has seldom been incorrect.

Managing Wicklow would be a massive challenge, even to the genius of Micko. There was little to lose and much to gain. In the early days there were moments when Arthur wondered if it would work. There would be glimmers of hope and then setbacks. After the first twenty minutes of the first of the three game saga against Louth in the 2007 Leinster Championship, Arthur recalls Micko turning to him and saying: "Win, lose or draw, we've the makings of a nice side here. We're onto something." There followed a replay and extra time in Parnell Park before Louth finally defeated Wicklow in the third match.

In 2007 and 2008 Wicklow, because they were a Division 4 side, were not permitted to use the qualifier series. Instead they competed in the Tommy Murphy Cup, a competition for "the weaker counties". Wicklow defeated Antrim after extra time to win this competition in 2007. In 2008 the same two teams met again in the final where Antrim gained revenge for the previous year. Arthur wonders where Wicklow would be now if the qualifiers had been open to the team for the previous two years.

The aim facing the team was to get off the 31st rung of the ladder. The only goal was to improve the overall standard of football and to bring a new-found interest to the county team. Arthur and Micko had many conversations about the state of Wicklow football. The Mayo man maintains that there was apathy in Wicklow towards the county team. Wicklow have one All Star, Kevin O'Brien, and Wicklow people often refer to this. Arthur reminds me that Mayo have not won an All Ireland in 50 years, but have won numerous All Star Awards. He wonders how many people could name the Mayo All Stars.

He maintains that Micko is always positive whereas Wicklow football has been malnourished on a diet of negativity. He recalls an incident during Hugh Byrne's chairmanship of Wicklow County Board. As usual Wicklow were losing at half time in the first round of the Leinster Championship. The chairman went into the dressing room and began his half time talk: "Come on now girls..." However there has been a huge change in the mindset of the Wicklow supporters. Monuments of defeat and negativity have had to be demolished.

I asked Arthur, after three years at the helm, if many of the aims which had been set had been met. He felt that once again there was a hint of the same old story with Wicklow following the Westmeath game. For most of the game Wicklow had Westmeath on the rack. We lost three defenders in the space of a few minutes to injury and another was sent off on a second yellow card close to the final whistle. In extra time Westmeath came out on top. There was much criticism of the Wicklow team following that defeat. Indeed in the media some harsh things were said about the team, and this match was televised live. However Wicklow made an incredible turn around. In the first qualifier against Fermanagh, Wicklow lost Tony Hannon to a second yellow card in the first half. With 60 minutes gone Thomas Walsh also received a second yellow. Yet the team showed its true mettle and beat the northern team.

I asked Arthur what he would say to those who believe that he and Micko are only in it for the money. Arthur replied that his involvement with Wicklow has actually cost him more than he has received. He has put his hand in his pocket on many occasions and was happy to do so.

However the whole economic climate of the country has changed in the last 12 months, and Arthur feels that were he to continue that he would not be able to be as generous. As regards whatever Micko has received, Arthur maintains that no one person has done as much for the GAA as Micko has and has received very little in return. How many bums has Micko put on seats over the years? Arthur tells me that Micko is probably the least monetary-minded person that he knows.

Micko is a non-smoker and a non-drinker, nor does he spend a huge amount on entertainment. Money means little to him. There are managers up and down the country who would be receiving much more than Micko in expenses. Micko never got fortunes from his involvement in Gaelic games. And what's more, Micko never looked for fortunes.

When asked if he would stay for another year, Arthur said that circumstances may well make it impossible. He certainly would like to stay on. The whole journey was among the most enjoyable and unbelievable experiences of his life. Arthur got to work with the greatest genius of all time in Gaelic football "and it doesn't get better than that." He met some of the best GAA people and the players were wonderful to work with. There were no incidents with any of them and they showed him total respect at all times. However the altered economic and commercial state of the country has impacted on Arthur. He made his livelihood from property, but today the banks are not lending any more. He shows me his mobile phone and said that up until last year that it would be continually hopping. I would have found it difficult to meet Arthur, but on this August morning when I am talking to him in his home in Kildare the phone only rings twice and Arthur gives me as much time as I need.

In O'Loughlin's Hotel following the defeat to Kildare, Arthur spoke to the assembled players and backroom team. He said that he was signing off that night and that it was going to be his last chance to address the entire panel together.

I asked him about the criticism that was made that no subs were used during the four qualifiers. He said that he addressed this issue in his speech when he said that no one wanted to come off during any of the four games. It would have been a most difficult call to make – every player was giving his all and they were fit. Who could be taken off? Wicklow were still in the game until Kildare scored the goal with just minutes left. He felt that there was no outstanding replacement available on the substitute bench, but that in time they will get their chance to make their mark.

Arthur had to think for a few moments when I asked him what his most memorable moment was during his three years. After much thought he said that the most outstanding moment was probably beating Kildare in Croke Park last year. It was the first time for Wicklow to win a championship match in Croke Park, but not only that, it was the style with which the team played. It was a comprehensive victory too. This year had numerous good moments – the standard of football that Wicklow played in the second half against Longford, and the manner in which the team refused to give up when Longford clawed their way back into the game in the closing minutes.

There was much harsh criticism of the team following the defeat to Westmeath. Tony Hannon had an off day, but when he rediscovered his confidence, what a difference he made. The Hollywood player was awarded the Vodafone Player of the month for July, particularly after his superb 45 in the dying moments against a strong wind which secured victory against Down. Nothing can replace a high octane championship match for a player.

Both Arthur and Micko believe that a light-hearted atmosphere makes a huge difference to a team, and therefore there was always much banter and joking at training. Winter training is drudgery enough. A little banter takes the hardship out of it. Indeed, it was often remarked that training was more like a circus than anything else.

Arthur's biggest regret? "Wicklow had fifty-eight per cent of the play against Kildare in the fourth round qualifier and still lost. That still hurts. Against Louth in 2007 Wicklow played three and a half matches and then had to exit the championship. Another downer was the loss to Laois last year in the second round of the championship."

Arthur believes that Kildare did not play as well against Tyrone as they did against us and yet only lost by a couple of points. Wicklow would have played well against Tyrone. Decisions went against Wicklow in the Kildare game, particularly during the second half.

He believes that the GAA are wonderful at paying lip service to "the weaker counties". He also believes that Mick O'Dwyer has been much maligned by referees.

Arthur tells me that during the two years in the Tommy Murphy Cup there were some great games. In one match Wicklow were trailing Offaly by seven points but managed to overcome the deficit. The 2007 final was a great game. Should the Tommy Murphy Cup be kept? Banishing Division 4 teams to this competition was not the most enlightened decision. After winning it the victors should have been allowed into the qualifiers the following year. Perhaps a team should be put into the Tommy Murphy Cup if they lose their first provincial championship match and their first qualifier.

Arthur said that he was as enthusiastic in year three as he was in year one with Micko and Wicklow. Did Arthur's involvement with the team have any negative impact on his family life? He said that it did not effect his family too much. He is a widower and the children are grown up. His daughter Arlene is a nutritionalist and dietician who would attend training sessions from time to time. The family would come to the matches too. "Micko has changed many people's lives. He makes gentlemen out of young men without them knowing it. He shows respect to everyone, child, teenager, adult or pensioner."

Arthur recalls a story that Niall Quinn related about Micko. Niall, as a child, was on holidays in Kerry in the 1980s. One day he and his father visited Micko's garage to see if they could get the maestro's autograph. Micko was in the pit working on a car and got out and disappeared into the house without saying a whole lot. The young Niall and his father thought that Micko was ignoring them and were about to leave the garage when he returned. The Kerryman apologised to them for leaving them in the garage but said that he had gone into the house to wash his hands as they were dirty and he did not want to soil the young boy's autograph book.

During my journey I realised that there was a huge amount of repetition – the same effort, the same pain, the same drills night in night out. Yet whenever Micko speaks it is almost as if you are hearing it for the first time. Although he often had the same message to give time after time, he never sounded repetitive or boring.

Arthur believes that simplicity is the secret of Micko's genius. Often he is criticised that he does hot have any large written plans. Yet Micko can replay almost every moment of a game. He can analyse in tremendous detail. Arthur explains that Micko brings a meticulous professionalism to training. His training methods have often been criticised as being old fashioned. The proof of the pudding is in the eating – look at his record in Kerry, Kildare and Laois. Look at what he achieved in Wicklow: a Tommy Murphy Cup victory, a first championship win in Croke Park and an appearance in the last twelve in this year's championship. Wicklow played six and a half games in seven weeks – they were still full of running after the final whistle.

Some counties are obsessed with weight training and gym work. Micko keeps it simple - lots of physical work during the winter and plenty of ball work when the evenings get longer. Once the clocks go forward it is time to play football. Arthur said that hardly a day would go by without at least one phone call from Micko, Martin Coleman or Jimmy Whittle. At times it seems that there was endless talk about the team, but it consumes you. Arthur managed the team for the 2007 Tommy Murphy Cup campaign while Micko was ill, and he enjoyed the experience thoroughly. Even if he had never managed the team for any length of time, he was happy to be number two or twenty-two. As long as he was involved with the team he was delighted. At one stage Arthur was a Maor Uisce but ended up being the cause of the county board being fined for some infringement. He was also the cause of another fine when he was found talking to Micko on the sideline when he should have been in the selectors' designated area.

Arthur told me that there were many times when there were requests and demands made of him, but that he never grew tired of trying to meet all commitments. At times it was difficult to squeeze everything in, and on occasion he had to miss training. "Missing training would kill me. It was a labour of love."

A little known fact was that Leighton Glynn was not fully fit before either the Down and Kildare games. The captain phoned Arthur and the selector made the journey to Mayo to collect some herbal remedies for the player. It was a similar story with Ciarán Hyland ahead of the Kildare game. The star defender had been suffering from a cold and once again Arthur provided the herbal remedies at very short notice.

Arthur then told me about what he would say to the fringe players. He can empathise with the subs because he sat on the bench during his own playing days. A sub does not mind seeing a player getting injured – it opens the door for him. He believes that everyone got a fair chance with Micko. Teams were selected on how players performed in training. There is only one place where all arguments are settled and that is on the field of play. There are two stages to staking a claim on the county panel – by playing well for your club and by putting in the effort in training.

The standard of competitive football within the county must improve. He then cites the example of the Kilkenny hurling panel where training matches are often more competitive than many an inter-county game. Playing As against Bs is a vital element of training. There are many members of the Kilkenny panel who never get to warm up their legs in a competitive match. There needs to be at least thirty-five players on the panel and every one of them has a vital role to play. Number thirty-five has as valuable contribution to make as any other player. Without substitutes there is no competition.

As my time with Arthur comes to an end I ask him about Fr. Tom O'Brien, a Corkman, and a Cistercian friar who died earlier this year in his eighties. Through Martin McAleese, husband of President Mary McAleese, Arthur was able to stay in the monastery in Portlanone. Monastic life has always fascinated Arthur, and it was during his stay in the monastery that he got to know Fr. Tom. Such was the friendship that developed, Fr. Tom often stayed in Arthur's house. Fr. Tom was chaplain in Our lady's Manor in Dalkey in recent years and is was during this time that he became the unofficial chaplain to the team. He would often attend training and would bless the team before they travelled to a game. During his final illness earlier this year, Jimmy Whittle arranged for the panel to sign a get-well card for him. On his death-bed Fr. Tom's proudest possession was this card and he would get visitors to read the card for him.

Arthur wanted to emphasise the extraordinary contributions both Martin Coleman and Jimmy Whittle had made to the team. There were never any difficulties with requests and expenses were never queried. Jimmy always had everything in order whether at training in Knockananna on a winter's evening or at the height of the championship. All in all it was a fantastic backroom team.

KEVIN O'BRIEN

Kevin O'Brien is Wicklow's one and only All Star winner. He began playing for the county team at U-14 level when he was just 12 years old, and played senior football for 15 years. He won a Railway Cup medal with Leinster in 1986, and a Club All Ireland with Baltinglass in 1989. He also toured Australia with the Compromise Rules team later that year and was named full forward on the 1990 All Stars Team. Being from Baltinglass, Kevin is next to the Kildare border. In 1998 he wondered if he had declared for Kildare would he have been on an All Ireland winning team? But Kevin is a Wicklowman through and through.

O'Brien believes that not enough was done to build on the solid base which had been put down in the 1986-91 period. He believes too few people in Wicklow actually believed in the county team, an attitude that infuriated him. There were times, too, when a lack of ambition permeated through to the players, with the result that some didn't always show enough commitment to the cause. O'Brien was different. The

greater the disappointment, the greater the challenge; the bigger the problem, the bigger the need for a solution.
(*The Chosen Ones: Celebrating 1000 GAA All Stars* by Martin Breheny and Colm Keys, Dublin: Blackwater Press, 2004, p. 144)

I met Kevin at his house in Baltinglass. Although he was in the middle of major home improvements, he took time out to chat to me for whatever length of time I wanted. He lent me his copy of the Chosen Ones and said that much of the background information that I would need was in this. My first question to him was how he had come into county management. He told me that he had been approached to train the St. Patrick's team in Tullow. There were many difficulties facing him, such as players playing soccer, rugby and socialising, so it was a matter of learning fast. He stayed with St. Patrick's for two years after which he took a two year break from football. In 2006 he received a phone call from Micko and he had no hesitation in accepting the position of trainer.

When Micko took over at the helm morale was very low. The team had been beaten by Carlow in Wexford Park in the first round of the qualifiers in 2006. Micko insisted that if he were going to do this job that he was going to do it his way and that he expected full support from the county board. All clubs were invited to send players along to the preliminary training sessions. At the first of these 121 players showed up. Over the next few months some pulled out and others were not deemed to be inter-county standard. However, every player who turned up was given a fair chance and some were given second chances.

In January 2007 Wicklow won their first two O'Byrne Cup matches before falling to Dublin. However the three matches were played in Aughrim and each of them was shown live on television. This was more live televised games in two weeks than Kevin had played in during his fifteen year inter-county career. There were huge numbers at these three games and it was a learning experience for the panel. It also helped the players to get used to playing in front of the cameras, something that was almost unheard of in Wicklow.

Will Kevin O'Brien stay on? Of course that is up to the county board to decide. Certainly if Micko were to stay Kevin would stay. Micko always stressed the bigger picture, that is, the players. Drills in training must have a purpose. Micko's methods have worked; eight All Irelands with Kerry, two Leinster titles with Kildare and one with Laois, not to mention numerous Munster titles and National Leagues. According to Kevin, Micko is like a father figure whose overriding principle is to do the right thing. Micko brought a vast store of knowledge with him to Wicklow, and Arthur French. According to Kevin, not only was Arthur an important member of the backroom staff, but his contributions were vital.

Like anyone connected with this Wicklow team Kevin O'Brien has many memories. Perhaps the greatest memory of his is the steady progress that was made over the three years. He believes that footballers are similar to racehorses. Some horses race better in heavy conditions. Some players shine in the league when underfoot conditions are often heavy to say the least. Other players come into their own once the evenings lengthen and the ground dries up.

Breaking the Croke Park hoodoo by beating Kildare was a big highlight of the three years as was winning the silverware in headquarters. Travelling to matches with a garda escort was breaking new ground for Wicklow and made the players feel good about themselves. Another highlight from Micko's three years was the change in attitude among the players. Players now want to play for Wicklow which was not always the case. The main aim of the first year was to get fit and to build on this fitness in subsequent years. Micko proved that it can be done. All he asked for from the players was honesty. According to Kevin, Micko is the fairest person he has ever worked with or under. For Micko the players were always the number one priority. At all times the backroom team respected the confidentiality of the dressing room and training pitch. Kevin found that as part of the management team he was reluctant to socialise. This was one of the sacrifices of being on the management team - you had to remain distant and intensely private about the job.

Kevin biggest regret was whenever a good young player pulled out of the panel. Being involved in an inter-county team involves a huge commitment, whether as player, mentor or official. However he has no big regrets from his own involvement with the team because everyone gave of their best, from the county board right down to those who cleaned the changing rooms and every else in between. That was not the way when Kevin was playing for the county. One slight disappointment which Kevin still feels occurred on the day when Wicklow won the Tommy Murphy Cup. Officious stewards did not permit the team to do a lap of honour. As is often the case in GAA circles, officialdom can spoil an historic day with its precocious adherence to the letter of the law. Surely it's the spirit and not the letter of the law that really counts?

The Tommy Murphy Cup victory certainly helped Wicklow. However Kevin felt that once a county won the Tommy Murphy Cup they should have been allowed to play in the following year's qualifiers. Surely this would have been an incentive to "the weaker counties"? On the day of the Tommy Murphy Cup the match began at midday and it was also played on a Saturday. However unsatisfactory these arrangements may have been, at least Wicklow got to play in a final in Croke Park. They gained valuable experience which did help the following year when they defeated Kildare at the same venue. There followed a trip to New York later that year when every member of the travelling party was kitted out in a suit. It was almost like being a Premiership team going to play a Champions League match. That good feeling was brought back to the clubs by the players upon their return.

Kevin's response to not using subs during the four match run was as follows: During the Westmeath game we lost three first-choice defenders. Four players also pulled out of the panel following this defeat. That is seven players gone in one go. Kevin would not do anything different if he were faced with the same choices now. He agreed totally with Micko and Arthur. Who would they have taken off during any of the four qualifiers? Everyone of the fifteen players gave their all and could not have given any more to the effort. Following the Westmeath game we were down seven experienced players. Would it have been fair to put a young inexperienced player into the cauldron of a knock-out championship game? What if the young player were not ready for that leap in standard? What would the effect on his confidence be? A substitute is only one match away from a fabulous career. John McGrath was probably the most likely substitute who might have been used, but he was not championship fit at the time, only coming back from a broken collar bone. However, Kevin expects that all county players should stand out for their clubs in the county championship. Brian Lennon, who came back to the panel mid championship, has shone for his club Donard.

Kevin was asked if there were ever a time when he was tempted to quit the backroom. Last year his wife Catherine got sick and it was a difficult time for the family. He pushed himself harder at training and consequently the team too. Both Arthur and Micko were aware of Kevin's situation and were understanding and supportive of his plight. Like the author, this journey with the Wicklow footballers was a journey of self-discovery. Thankfully Catherine is making a full recovery and his children have had a fantastic year following Wicklow. He tells me that his youngest daughter asked him recently if Micko was leaving Wicklow. Little Áine wants Micko to stay.

Travelling for Kevin was not a big problem. He would travel with Noel Molloy and Martin Coleman from Baltinglass to training. During the first year of Micko's reign, training moved from club to club. Everywhere there was a wonderful reception for the county team. The welcome from the Knockananna club stands out as being most memorable.

Also during this first year Micko attended countless medal presentations. At every presentation the recipients were made feel as if they had just won a senior All Ireland. The support and goodwill that was generated can be measured in the increased numbers who attended championship matches whenever Wicklow were playing. The qualifier matches against Down and Kildare were also broadcast live on television.

Kevin hopes that Micko will stay. "I lost one father already this year. I don't want to lose another," he tells me. But the county needs more talented players. Like Jack Charlton, Kevin believes in the grandparent rule. Unfortunately not too many quality players have discovered that they have Wicklow grandparents. Thomas Walsh came to Wicklow and made a huge contribution to the success of the team. However he lost his job, as many players the length and breadth of the country have in recent months, and he was forced to return home. For Micko and Arthur people matter. Neither of these two men need the money – both are successful businessmen. The bigger picture for them is to get players to compete and to push themselves to newer heights.

As a revenue collector for Wicklow County Council Kevin's job involves looking for money. However during the run in the qualifiers people forgot about the recession and the feel good factor was palpable. Kevin said that he took some of Arthur's herbs himself and found that they gave him an energy boost. The energy boost that these herbs gave saw Wicklow through many a tough final ten minutes, especially against Fermanagh and Down.

Over the years Wicklow football was content to accept what might have been. O'Brien, even as a player, never accepted the moral victory attitude. "Moral victories are bullshit. If and but never won anything." Honesty in training is what wins matches. Micko did push the players hard, but there was always good banter among the panel. Fun comes after winning and winning becomes a habit you want to keep. It was this honest attitude to training that helped Kevin through a difficult year. He reminds me of the attitude before the Kildare qualifier. When the Wicklow players were warming up on the training pitch there was a relaxed attitude. There was a bit of banter and light heartedness, but the focus was still on the game. When the Kildare players came out onto the training pitch one could almost feel the stress and tension that they were feeling. That relaxed attitude is what Micko brings to a team. Before each game he would tell the players to go out and enjoy themselves, that there was no point in worrying or becoming stressed out and that it was just another game of football. O'Brien is adamant that this attitude of Micko gets you the fifteen players you can trust on the pitch.

There are always opportunities for players to break into a team. Against Westmeath Wicklow lost three players. Dean Odlum must surely have been tempted to quit on many occasions. When he joined the panel he was not fit and suffered in training. He sat on the subs' bench for a long time, but when he got into the team he held onto his place for dear life. His name was a household name during the glorious voyage of the qualifiers of 2009. O'Brien thinks that it is regrettable that any player would refuse Micko's invitation to make a name for himself. Players are unemployed, but training gives them a goal during the day. Often it was the player who had no job who was first to training and worked the hardest.

O'Brien cannot criticise Micko's training methods. The principle is to get fit and play football. This view of Micko's is not followed by everyone. At one stage there were six of the seven U-21s who were on the panel with injuries to the hamstring or groin. Most of these players were training with their colleges. Micko also believes that the long runs make the players mentally strong. Kevin introduced medicine ball drills and some boxing-type training during the winter sessions in order to add a bit of variety to the sessions. Micko accepted this. When Micko took over Wicklow he was well aware of the county's reputation with regard to discipline. He was of the opinion that it would take three or four months to sort out the discipline issues. Hopping the ball once a player received it was something that took a lot longer to rectify.

One night Kevin was approached by Ciarán Hyland whose mother was ill. The player who had a tremendous season was tempted to find consolation in pints of beer, and Kevin related his own experience. Ciarán trained harder and went to the gym during his lunch break. What a season the corner back had!

I also asked Kevin if he ever got fed up with the demands which were placed on him. Not at all: three teams have approached Kevin to train them. People in Wicklow are beginning to see the bigger picture. They now know what it takes to be successful. Whatever happens in the next few years, we must never let this momentum slip. The county got on the Micko bandwagon this year and had a ball. There was pride and success in Wicklow football for a change. The key to all of this was Micko and Arthur. He showed the panel the value of positive thinking. These two men had nothing to prove to anyone. Both were successful business and both had achieved success in Gaelic football. Yet they have a passion and they have ignited a fire in the belly of every Wicklow supporter. The players are the most important element in any team. Micko and Arthur raised the bar. For this Wicklow will forever be grateful.

As I am leaving Kevin he brings me into the sitting room and hands me his All Star Award. He said: "I don't want to be Wicklow's only All Star. By the end of the year I want Ciarán Hyland and Leighton Glynn to have one each, and in Leighton's case it's long overdue." Both players received nominations, but unfortunately neither Wicklowman won the coveted award. However Kevin has been appointed as selector with the International Rules team for 2010 and 2011.

PHILIP MacGILLICUDDY

Philip MacGillicuddy is from An Tochar GAA Club in Roundwood, supposedly the highest village in Ireland. He has played for Wicklow at all levels from U-14 upwards. In 1987 at the age of 18 he played minor and U-21 for the county. That October he played senior in the league in the time when the leagues were played either side of Christmas. He ended his inter-county career in the late nineties and continued to play for his club until 2002. In 2003 and 2004 he managed his own club and for the next two years he managed the Kilinerin club in Wexford. In 2007 he joined the Wicklow management team.

Philip had been a selector with the U-21s in 1999 and 2000. Seán Mulryan's sons were on the team and Philip is of the opinion that Billy Timmons, who was instrumental in bringing Arthur and Micko to Wicklow, may have suggested Philip to them. Philip's father is Dónal MacGillicuddy, a former chairman of Wicklow county board. He is also a Kerryman. When Philip was approached to join the management team it was not a complete shock to him and he had no hesitation in accepting.

Following Wicklow's loss to Carlow in Wexford Park in 2006, morale in the football camp was at, yet, another, all-time low. Micko asked Philip to manage the U-21s with a view to establishing a supply line to the senior team. In October 2006 following the appointment of the Micko management team, Philip's first priority was to look at the players who were available for U-21 duty. This meant the he did not spend a whole lot of time thinking about the seniors but rather was concentrating on focusing on the age-limit team.

In his first year as U-21 manager seven players were given a chance with the seniors, in the second year ten and in 2009, thirteen players were called up. Not all of these players graduated to the senior ranks, but at least the supply line was running.

With regard to what has been achieved over the three years of Micko's reign, Philip says it was an eye-opener for the players. Some failed to make the grade while others blossomed under Micko. Over the three years more than two hundred players were given the chance to try out for the county team. It was glaringly obvious that what used pass for intercounty requirements in Wicklow was no longer acceptable.

The second comment that Philip made was that the gap between club and county has widened. Time is required to adapt to the step up in standard from club to county. Micko often reminded the squad of the Kerry players who had to sit on the bench for some years before getting their chance. When they did get their opportunity they grabbed it and held on to it for dear life. Some of these Kerry players then went on to win All Irelands and All Star Awards. It was an entirely new concept for a Wicklow player to have to bide his time. The era of the "I can come and go attitude" of the Wicklow player had come to an end.

When asked if he would stay on for another term as selector Philip said that he would have no hesitation in doing so as long as Micko was still at the helm. This year was particularly difficult for Philip due to work commitments, but he found the manager to be very understanding.

I asked Philip about not using any substitutes in the qualifiers and he replied that he had no complaints about this. "Only make a change when it's going to make an improvement" is the guiding principle of Micko on making substitutions. If you trust a player to start you must give him the chance to prove himself. The fifteen players who played in the four qualifiers all had depths of reserves. The Wicklow panel is very young and it would have been unfair on a new player to put them on in the cauldron of championship. Against Longford and Westmeath subs were used: some of them worked out and some did not. Although there were many memorable moments during this three year voyage with Micko, Philip thinks that the feeling of euphoria when the final whistle sounded in the Down match was the sweetest sound of all. We beat a good Down team playing quality football. But there were other great memories: winning the Tommy Murphy Cup in 2007 and beating our neighbours Kildare in Croke Park were also memorable occasions. Another highlight was the second drawn match, after extra time, against Louth in the 2007 Leinster Championship. That was the first time that Philip ever heard the chant "Wicklow! Wicklow!" at a match.

Philip wonders if the best people are in the right positions across the board. Structures must be right if a county is to succeed, and he cites the example of Kerry where it appears that the best people are in the top positions.

Philip agrees that the Tommy Murphy Cup fulfilled its purpose when Wicklow won it in 2007. He feels that there was little to be gained from winning it in 2008. It had fulfilled its purpose and in a way had retarded progress as we were not permitted to play in the qualifiers. When he looks at the progress that was made in this year's qualifiers he cannot help but wonder what might have been had we been allowed entry to the 2008 series. Micko always made you feel that progress had been made at every training session and that the potential was coming close to being realised. In short, training was genuinely enjoyable.

Philip is blessed in that his wife comes from a GAA family. His wife knew what the commitment required was, although it has to be said, that with a young child it was not always easy. However this summer was a reward for all those family members who made tremendous sacrifices over the last three years. On the business front Philip had just begun a new venture in January and his involvement in county management did add some pressure, especially when there would be meetings that had to be attended but that clashed with training. However Micko, as always, was very understanding and if his selector could not make training it was never an issue.

Micko's genius is his simplicity. Winter training is difficult, but it weeds out those who are not committed and lack the required determination to play for the county. It builds up a player's character and helps to develop a spirit in the camp. Also, few of Micko's players suffer from long-term injuries. Come the long evenings he plays attractive football in a good atmosphere. Philip feels that criticism of the team's performance was justified following the defeat to Carlow in the league this year. Wicklow supporters travelled to see the team and they were disappointed. Philip feels that it was fair that they let off steam. However, it's a long road and supporters cannot always see the whole plan. Criticism is part and parcel of life. The worst thing you can do is to let it get in on you. Accept it and move on. Micko's record: participation in over twenty All Ireland finals at some level and provincial titles with three different counties. Wicklow have never even won a Leinster senior championship.

"Micko," said Philip, "was always fair." There was a reasonable number of players between the ages of eighteen and twenty who were invited to come to training. There is a huge step up from club standard to Micko's requirements and those players who stuck with it did well to stay. Micko has always been open and honest with regard to how he selects his starting fifteen. He has told the squad that if they are not selected this time there are always opportunities in the future. He cites the examples of Darren Hayden, Stephen 'Chester' Kelly and Brian McGrath who all got their chance in the first qualifier match and continued to hold down their places until the final whistle of the fourth and final match. Being selected is sometimes all about timing. Players can see what is required and what they have to do if called upon. Philip still has some doubts as to whether or not Wicklow had their best thirty. He thinks that there is still room for improvement and can only imagine what will happen when that day comes.

To change the fortunes of Wicklow, he says he would change the structure of the club championship. Of the sixteen teams that are currently playing senior football in Wicklow, he feels that only half of these are really senior standard. In Kerry where success is almost a God-given right, they have teams made from groups of clubs. He feels that four average junior clubs could possibly make a good senior side and in this way every adult who is close to senior standard would have the opportunity to play senior football. He feels that lack of top class competition at club level is holding back the county. He cites the number of players on the Cork starting fifteen who are playing club football at junior level, yet can make the grade at county level. He does not feel that club versus county is a problem any more in the county and believes that club rivalry is healthy, but there still needs to be a balance. He thinks that the club championship should be played earlier in the summer. Philip knows what some of the bad ol' days were like.

He feels that junior and intermediate clubs have inhibited the development of the GAA in Wicklow because of the claims that the senior championship interferes with their set up. Wicklow has a history of good people leaving – it is time to get them to the top table where their vision and enthusiasm cannot but improve the GAA in Wicklow at every level.

If next year were not to be as good or even better than this year there is the fear that the county would slip back to the loosing pattern of yesteryear. He ponders football in Wicklow without Micko – how would the panel react to a new manager? What is needed is a clear plan. Dublin hurling has made tremendous advances in recent years, so much so, that they are now second only to Kilkenny in Leinster. This is no accident. Dublin put massive resources into coaching and games development at underage level. Starting at primary school and underage, Dublin invested heavily in developing hurling with the youngest players. That investment is now paying dividends, even though there were some set backs along the way – and all of that in a county which is known as a footballing county. Where there is a will there is a way.

GERRY FARRELL

Gerry Farrell is a Wicklow Town man and has been a lifelong member of the St. Patrick's Club where he both played and managed. Although he was not involved with the county team during this glorious year, he was a selector during Micko's first two years. At first he was reluctant to talk to me as he felt that he was not part of the set up in 2009. He eventually relented when I assured him that without his contribution during 2007 and 2008 that 2009 would not have happened. He was part of the management team with his club between 2002 and 2006. For ten years, between 1992 and 2002 he managed Kilenerin. Between 1984 and 1989 he managed St. Patrick's and he was involved with the county team in 1989 and 1990. With Michael Sargent and Peter O'Neill, Gerry was part of the U-21 set up between 1985 and 1990. Indeed Gerry was a selector when a Wicklow team which had Kevin O'Brien and Philip MacGillicuddy playing defeated Kildare in Aughrim.

Gerry was first approached by Billy Timmons to consider coming on board after the county final in 2006 which St. Pat's won. Because of his club commitment, Gerry asked for some time to consider his position. In the Leinster Championship Kildare's Moorefield defeated St. Patrick's and ended his club's involvement in the championship. It was too good an opportunity to turn down, and as Micko was committing to Wicklow for two years, Gerry would do likewise. Once on board Gerry saw that this was the best opportunity ever for Wicklow to make substantial progress. There was a huge reaction to Micko's arrival in the county. A huge number of players turned up to the early training sessions. The initial difficulty was to reduce this number to between forty and fifty by Christmas 2006. At training there was a huge buzz - players from smaller clubs were getting an opportunity to try out for the county. How to filter out those who would not make the grade was easier said than done. What Micko brought to Wicklow was a massive enthusiasm and optimistic outlook that was never here before.

Gerry said he regarded the highlight of his two years as the winning of the Tommy Murphy Cup in 2007. In fact when Gerry spoke about it he became a little emotional. Wicklow at last had won a trophy in Croke Park – many a Wicklow player had played and lost there. He remarked that it was unbelievable to see the pride of his own people that day in Croke Park. That victory brought a new degree of respectability to Wicklow. The match was shown live on television and it was a most exciting game that had extra time and Wicklow scoring the winning goal in the dying seconds. Another highlight was the victory over Kildare in the 2008 championship. In the following game against Laois he felt that the team was very unlucky. During the second half of that game the team played at a new level. There was a marked increase in the pace of the game. The team had moved up a gear from 2007 and it was a huge disappointment to lose that match. To be playing at that increased pace and level means that your team is going places. This year Gerry noticed that at the VHI Cúl Camps in his own club there was only one child who was not wearing either a club, Cúl Camp or county GAA shirt. Not too long ago the children would have been wearing any number of Premiership jerseys. This, he feels, is part of the effect that Micko has had on the county: a county with pride in itself.

With regard to the biggest disappointments, without doubt the defeat to Laois was the biggest. That night in Carlow the team played extremely well, especially in the second half. Luck did not go the Wicklow Way. There were goal chances that the woodwork denied. Gerry believes that had the game ended in a draw Wicklow would have won in extra time or in a replay. He believes that the performance that night laid down a marker: Wicklow were capable of taking the game to anyone.

Although Wicklow did not progress from Division 4 during the three years of Micko's reign, the manager never made any secret that he was preparing the team for the championship. From the very first training session that Micko took, his emphasis was always was that the team had one date and that was 18th May 2007 against Louth. Every year it is the same with Micko: what counts is the championship.

CHAPTER SIX

Let The
Games Begin!

THE month of May is upon us again. The Championship is only three weeks away. There is no hiding place now. Bring on Longford on Sunday 24th.

SATURDAY 2ND MAY
Training in Aughrim

Glorious sunshine bathes the Aughrim pitch. The mood is upbeat. Damian Power is waiting to enter "Noels' Parlour of Pain" as he calls the treatment table. He is having his two ankles taped up and I remark that if he weren't taped up that he would fall apart. The Rathnewman quips back that he is sponsored by Elastoplast!

Kevin takes the warm-up which consists of some jogging and stretching exercises. There follows some faster runs across and back the pitch. There is a series of sprints to the 13 and 20 metre lines. The players must start from the crouch position and should be going a full speed as they cross the finish line. I am slightly surprised that everyone appears to slow down before the finish line. There follows a series of 50 press-ups. Much to Kevin's disgust some of the panel are struggling with them. These are inter-county players. They should be doing at least 50 press-ups at home every day. Tony Hannon jokes that they are too slow and is rewarded with counting a fast set of 30. Kevin is by far the best of the squad and gets up after the 30th as if he had merely been calling them out rather than doing them. Micko stresses the importance of physical fitness. He says, "We want to run these Longford fellas off the pitch". There follows a fast run in groups of six from the end line around the far goal to finish at the near twenty-one. Dean Odlum is first to finish. Dean had been one of the most unfit members of the squad when he joined two years ago but has worked hard to achieve a level of fitness few would have thought possible.

Micko calls on Arthur to demonstrate some place kicking. He is given four footballs and told to put them over the bar from the edge of the semi-circle. He misses the first two. The payers good naturedly jeer him and say it's not so easy when there are a few thousand watching you from the stands. Arthur responds by putting over four in a row. Earlier on this morning he kicked 30 one after the other, none from inside the 20 metre line. As he said himself, not bad for a 61-year-old. Five steps are all he takes. Micko comments: "It's all about technique."

There is a 10-minute game of reds against yellows and once again there is neither soloing nor hopping allowed. Later on this ban is lifted. Micko's opinion is that hopping and soloing slows you down. His philosophy is as soon as you get the ball offload it to a better placed player. Keep the head up and always be looking for someone to pass it to.

Thomas Walsh is not training – he has a slight thigh strain and was on the treatment table. He does some light jogging with Ciarán Walsh but leaves early. Dara Ó hAnnaidh is back and takes a full part in training. The session finishes with a set of three sprints to the 45-and back to the 13 metre line followed by some cool-down exercises.

SUNDAY 3RD MAY
Training in Aughrim

Yesterday Leinster defeated the favourites Munster in the semi-final of the Heineken Cup. Over 82,000 attended the game in Croke Park, a world record attendance for a club rugby game. Earlier on this morning Ricky Hatton was defeated by Manny Pacquiao in the MGM Grand Garden Arena Las Vegas. One or two of the squad who watched the fight live are feeling the effects of lack of sleep.

It is a bright morning but there is a bite to the wind. Thomas Walsh is not present and Kevin O'Brien works with Ciarán Walsh. Time is starting to run out for the young Baltinglass forward. He may be recovering from his hamstring injury, but he has missed out on a lot of training. There is a warm-up followed by a 70-minute 13-a-side match of reds against yellows. At half-time Micko urges the half-backs not to be getting caught out going forward. Football must be quick and fast. The no hopping no soloing rule is applied for most of the game. "Fast and quick. Get the ball and release it." Dara O hAnnaidh opts out of the second half. He played a full part yesterday but today is feeling a bit sore. The reds are too strong for the yellows. Paul Earls is back from England and scores some good points. However he is facing into two weeks of exams so he won't be training with the squad again. Johnny Kinch pulls up after a tackle and is holding his back. He is brought into the treatment room where Prem thinks that there may be some damage to a disc. Dr. Cuddihy is contacted.

There was to be training tomorrow night, the bank holiday Monday on the beach in Brittas Bay but the selectors decide to give the panel the night off. Training will resume on Tuesday.

TUESDAY 5TH MAY
Training in Aughrim

Tonight it's very blustery and overcast. There does not appear to be a huge turn-out on the pitch. This is confirmed when Martin states that there are twenty on the pitch but that all other players have been accounted for. Two are playing in a colleges' final, one is doing exams, another is working and the rest are injured. I sense a certain lack of interest tonight. This surprises me because it is less than three weeks to the opening round of the championship. Do these players really believe that they can take Wicklow further than any other Wicklow team in the 125 year history of the GAA?

Are they lethargic because of the long weekend just gone? There are the usual warm-up laps, ladder work, soloing and fist passing drills. Jimmy Whittle remarks that there would be more players at an intermediate training session in his home club of Dunlavin. Kevin O'Brien remarks on how sluggish the panel is this evening. Micko calls the players together and demonstrates how he wants them to hold onto the ball, "Get it into the chest. Out there it'll be knocked out of your hands. Pull it into your chest. Don't be casual and drive in." There follows a series of sprints. Once again I am amazed that no player is going at full speed as they pass the finish line. They all seem to be pulling up short. I feel that this is a bad omen.

THURSDAY 7TH MAY
Training in Aughrim

Today I went to visit Hazel Devine, the bio-energy awareness expert whom the team met on Good Friday. Remarkably, she is able to tell me about various aspects of my past and present. It's as if she is able to see my thoughts and into my body. I am usually very sceptical about practices such as this. All I can say is go and see this woman. I come away from my appointment feeling thoroughly rejuvenated. She did a number of energy exercises with me and I feel fresh and ready to face the road to Aughrim and another night's training. For the first time I realize that this task of following the Wicklow footballers is not really about them and their season alone. This project has become a journey of self-discovery.

Because of my appointment in Tullamore I am late for training. Yet again I miss an opportunity. An RTÉ crew was in Aughrim earlier on to take some footage and to speak to Micko about the upcoming championship. When I get to Aughrim; the wind is blowing with quite a force. The squad has gone upstairs for their meal when the heavens open up. Micko leaves early as he is driving back to Waterville tonight for a funeral in the morning. It is a dirty night. We are amazed at the energy of this man of 72 who can take a training session and then drive 250 miles home in darkness and heavy rain. Arthur remarks, and not for the first time: "The bigger the challenge the more he rises to it." Are there any bigger challenges in Gaelic football than trying to bring Wicklow to the top table? Tomorrow night Micko will receive yet another hall of fame award - his fourth. Jokingly he said that he didn't know why they were giving it to him. "I'm not dead yet," he jokes.

As Jimmy is locking up, he remarks that unless Wicklow do something this year that there will be a whole new set-up next year. He is pleased that during the three seasons since Micko came on board that every player who is capable of playing inter-county football has been given the chance. The best fifteen are almost ready.

SATURDAY 9TH MAY
Minor Football Championship
After a most disappointing outing against Kildare in the opening round of the Leinster Championship, the minors have a comprehensive victory over Kilkenny. That's two victories in a row. Now they are back on track. Unfortunately the ladies' team is defeated in the Division Three final of the league.

SUNDAY 10TH MAY (LÁ NA gCLUB)
Training in Aughrim
Two weeks to go ... then it's do-or-die for this squad and their mentors. It is a beautiful morning. There is the usual practice match - reds against yellows. Some of the injured players are watching. John McGrath has his arm out of the sling and is hoping for good news when he goes for an x-ray tomorrow. Leighton Glynn has bruised ribs and is not playing. Brian McGrath is participating in a county training session for the first time since he came off injured in the London game at the end of March. Thomas Walsh is on the treatment table for shin splints but is making good progress.

From the dug-out I sense an intensity that has not been there before. Guys are hitting each other with force. Cathal McNicholas goes to ground and for a brief moment there was a fear that he had been badly hurt. Luckily he is alright and can resume. Paddy Dalton has laid down a marker. He wants to be a first choice player. This morning he is taking no prisoners. Paddy is not the tallest player on the pitch but he has plenty of heart and guts. He is not one to pull out of a challenge.

At the end of the game Micko calls the two teams together. "Now look lads," he begins, "I want to ask you a question. Are ye interested in playing for Wicklow? This morning we said we'd start at 11. Usually it's half ten. I have never in my life seen the likes of this – straggling in at the last minute. This is not about Kevin O'Brien or Philip or Arthur or me. This is about you. Now look lads, your attitude must change. Half seven on Tuesday means ten past seven. It doesn't mean straggling in and waiting to be last to get a rub. I never saw that at county or club level before. In Kerry, Declan O'Sullivan is seen doing laps of the pitch every morning at half seven. You're the very same. Ye all have two legs and two arms. What's lacking here is effort. In your spare time, you should be kicking football. Look lads, there are twenty-four hours in a day. If you spend half an hour kicking that still gives you twenty-three and a half hours to do whatever else you want to do.

"Kilkenny hurlers are out on the pitch pucking around every spare minute they have. One thing that's most important: catching. Eyes open. There're only two weeks left. It's up to you to achieve for Wicklow. Total commitment is what's needed. Look at Paddy Dalton. He cleaned out guys today. Tackle with your eyes open. Now we're going to practice the basic things for the next two weeks. Continue to do light weights. No heavy weights. There are plenty of gyms the length and breadth of Wicklow. Use them. Every chance you have get a ball and kick. Now that's all I've to say. See you on Tuesday ready to start at half past seven." With that the session breaks up.

I give Jimmy a hand to gather up footballs and other pieces of equipment. As I go to give Tony Hannon his top I discover that players are in the inner dressing room behind closed doors. I go in but decide to leave immediately. It would seem that all is not well. Some of the senior players are none too pleased with the casual attitude that has crept into training with only two weeks left to the championship. I wonder if there will be a change in attitude on Tuesday.

TUESDAY 12TH MAY
Training in Aughrim

There is a big turn out on the pitch by 7.20. Arthur tells me that he is slightly disappointed that Wicklow didn't make the break through that he thought they would under Micko. He believes that a lack of inter county success and a mindset of failure has led to an air of negativity within the county. Some of the players will not take the herbal energy solutions that have been provided for the team because they do not like the taste. The bio-energy specialist, Hazel Devine, found the energy levels of the team to be very low. Arthur believes that the players did not really understand what Hazel was about. Games are won and lost in the final ten minutes of a close match. Energy levels are vital. He believes that Seánie Furlong is potentially the best all round footballer but he is far from fully fit. Kevin who is forty-one and has a bad knee can still outrun him. The players had a meeting on Sunday last about their time-keeping and discipline. There is one thing talking about it on a Sunday, but it is another thing to do something about it. However there is progress tonight with the extra effort being put in to be out on the pitch ready to start the session at half seven.

Brian McGrath hobbles off during the practice match. He had not been running well during the warm-up. This is a worry. Both Thomas Walsh and Leighton Glynn are not participating in the game. Paddy Dalton is taking the 45s. He is a place-kicker for his club, Coolkenno, and he is not too far off the pace tonight. In goal Mervyn Travers is in fantastic form. Mervyn often finds the running difficult but when in goal he is practically unbeatable on a low shot. I wonder why players try to score goals on him when there are points for the taking?

At half-time Micko talks about the positioning of our half-backs for the kick outs. Arthur then speaks. He asks: "You have the greatest living legend here training you. Why is Wicklow down all the days? Your energy levels are low. We have the best stuff for you and you won't take it. This is outrageously disappointing. You're giving excuses like children: 'I don't like the taste'. If this was in Micko's Kerry, they'd eat grass! Act like inter county players. That's what you are."

After the final whistle the manager asks Martin Coleman to tell the players what the arrangements are for the next couple of weeks. There will be training on Thursday and Saturday morning in Aughrim. There will be a session in Portlaoise on Sunday morning and back to Aughrim on the following Tuesday and Thursday. The Longford game is Sunday week. There are numerous comments about "championship hair cuts" with Martin Coleman, Kevin O'Brien and Philip MacGillicuddy setting the standard. The final comment of the night is from Micko to Stephen Fanning: "How many cows to milk, Stephen?"

THURSDAY 14TH MAY
Training in Aughrim

As the training session begins the day-long rain stops, but it is quite misty and damp. There is no wind. After the warm up and stretches the players are put into groups of seven to run a fast lap. The last two home from each group will have to do another lap. Next there are the ladder drills. Kevin is concerned that with the championship only a week away the players are not bursting through the drills. He is looking for more enthusiasm. Mervyn is excellent at the ladder drills. I learn that this is from his time in England when he played with Sheffield United. In the practice match one hop or one solo is allowed. Unlike the drills earlier on in the evening, there is much more urgency about the practice match.

Mervyn talks to his team the whole way through the game. The comment is "Travers can be heard in the next parish." Kevin plays for one of the teams and the experience of the man can be seen. The whole way through the match he is coaching, coaxing and encouraging both sets of players. Defender Brian McGrath has been fighting to get fit. He participated fully in Tuesday's session but tonight he pulls up early in the match. It looks as if his ankle has not recovered and he has had a setback. Sunday week is slipping away. Brian is a big loss – this year he won a senior club championship with Kilmacud Crokes on St. Patrick's Day.

SATURDAY 15TH MAY
Training in Aughrim

I am in Croke Park attending a meeting of An Coiste Náisiúnta of Cumann na mBunscol. There are heavy showers and strong winds battering the country. This is also the weekend of the Irish Open Golf Championship in Baltray and play has been interrupted on more than one occasion due to the unfavourable weather conditions. Meanwhile in Aughrim the emphasis is on developing sharpness followed by a twenty-five minute game. With just one week to go the heavy work has been done. There is little more that can be done now.

SUNDAY 16TH MAY
Final Training Match in Portlaoise

Today, it is wet and cold. This is the middle of May and the weather is more like November. The football championship gets underway in earnest today: in Leinster, Louth take on Carlow in Parnell Park while Fermanagh have home advantage when they host Down in the Ulster Championship.

I arrive in Portlaoise at about 10.20 a.m. to find the panel togged out and the teams are just about to be announced. One team will wear the 2009 championship strip while the other team will wear the white strip. The blue team is as follows: Mervin Travers; Ciarán Hyland, Alan Nolan, Ciarán Doyle; Paddy Dalton, Dara Ó hAnnaidh, Padge McWalter; James Stafford, Thomas Walsh; Rory Nolan, Tony Hannon, Jacko Dalton; Dean Odlum, Seánie Furlong and Paul Earls. To me this looks like most of the team that will be starting next Sunday. Leighton Glynn is sitting out again today as are Seán Kinsella and Alan Byrne.

The white team is: Billy Norman; Anthony McLoughlin, Stephen "Chester" Kelly, Brian Osborne; Paddy Byrne, Stephen Fanning; Don Jackman, Shane Carthy; Darren Hayden, Pat Brophy, Niall Gaffney; Darragh O'Sullivan, Paul Cunningham and Ciarán Jones. Before the teams go out onto the pitch, Micko addresses the players. "Now lads, I'm not going to make a big speech. I want you to go out there and give it everything. We're going to pick the team today or on Tuesday. You'll know the team on Tuesday night. Is that right Martin?"

"That's right Micko," replies Martin.

The game is quite competitive. In a way it is quite surreal - after six months training there is only one week to go until the championship match against Longford. The weather is more like winter than mid-May. The blues are well in control. Billy Norman, the white's goalkeeper is absolutely furious with some of his team for their loose marking. By the time Micko blows the half-time whistle the blues are leading 3-10 to 0-4. If that could be the case next week ....

Micko instructs the two sets of forwards to change jerseys. The rest of the teams remain as they are and both teams continue to play into the same goals. His speech is briefer that the one in the changing room: "Play with determination, commitment and heart." Despite having the on-form forwards on their team, the whites fail to alter the result. The blues scored less but their backs were much busier than in the first half.

When the seventy minutes are up Micko calls the squad together on the pitch. He has little to say and invites Arthur to talk. Arthur says that the team is similar to where it was this time last year, a week before that famous victory over Kildare in Croke Park. Philip McGillicuddy is asked to say a few words. He commends the team, "we're getting there," but with a glint in his eye adds, "shameful refereeing!" "Micko replies, "The ref was top class!"

Breakfast is served in O'Loughlin's Hotel. This early afternoon it is a full-sized healthy fry and well deserved after a fairly competitive practice match. Declan O'Loughlin, the owner of the hotel shows us some photographs on the wall of the corridor leading to the function room. A few Wicklow players are among them and also Noel Molloy wearing his Rathvilly colours – complete with dark hair and 1980s style moustache. How times have changed!

Tonight The Sunday Game returns. This season Des Cahill is in the chair. This is the 125th anniversary year of the founding of the GAA and there is a feature with some of the greatest players from yesteryear reminiscing about their involvement in the GAA and some of their greatest memories. Joining Micko for this are Seán Boylan, Dermot Earley and Joe McKenna.

TUESDAY 19TH MAY
Training in Aughrim

There is a great buzz in Aughrim tonight. It is the week of the championship. This is what the months of training in the rain and wind and mud are all about. There are thirty-three players on the pitch. Someone remarks that in the days leading up to a championship match very few players need treatment. The manager calls the team together before the practice match begins. "We had to pick fifteen. We know there are fellas here who are as good. Look lads, we'll keep changing the subs to give everyone a fair chance."

Team captain Leighton Glynn is asked to say a few words. "Drive in," he urges. "Play the way we're going to play on Sunday." The game is ten minutes-a-side. There are sixteen on each team - three midfielders per team. The manager wants tight marking and that is what he gets. Hits are coming in fast and furious but fairly. The Waterville Maestro yells out: "That's the stuff! Tear into it." I am watching the game while sitting beside Kevin O'Brien in the dug out. He says: "Half of these lads wouldn't be here only for Micko. That has always been the way with Wicklow."

The game is very competitive. Some players who were not listed on the starting fifteen are playing exceptionally well. Micko remarks after the match, "We'll have to look at this team again. This is the one we'll give to the papers and we'll announce it on Sunday. We saw things tonight. You made a good impression and we'll have another good look at ye on Thursday. The way you were playing here tonight is the way I want you to play in Portlaoise. The B team was tearing into them. No matter where're you're playing, you have to fight and tackle for every ball. You have to say to yourself, 'Jesus, I'm gonna get that ball.' It's all about the work rate. We're surprised with some stuff here tonight. Now the team going to press is: Mervyn Travers; Ciarán Hyland, Alan Nolan, Alan Byrne; Padge McWalter, Dara Ó hAnnaidh, Paddy Dalton; Thomas Walsh, James Stafford; Tony Hannon, Leighton Glynn, Jacko Dalton; Dean Odlum, Seánie Furlong and Paul Earls. That may not be the team.

"Don't be offended if you're not on the team. We're picking the players who are in form. No player will be in on Sunday if he is not pulling his weight. Fire and brimstone - that's what we want. Lads, Portlaoise is a sandy pitch so make sure you have your screw-in studs. If anyone has a cold or flu ring the doc immediately. Don't be waiting until Sunday." And so the final countdown has begun.

THURSDAY 21ST MAY
Training in Aughrim

Today was the day of the golf classic in Blainroe Golf Club in aid of the football team. By all accounts it was a successful day. Training tonight is very low-key. Nobody wants to get injured at this stage after two hard training matches. Following the light work out the manager calls the players together.

"Right lads, on Sunday we're going to play our own game. We're not going to get bogged down in Longford's game. Wing forwards last Tuesday were atrocious - ye didn't tackle. We don't want to see forwards standing and watching play go by. Look lads, you're totally obsessed with soloing and then you run into trouble. Dara Ó hAnnaidh and Paddy Dalton we want you to play more defensively. Padge McWalter, you can go on a solo run if you have a clear pitch ahead of you. Midfielders attack when you can. James Stafford we want you in the square when there are frees against us. Tom, don't be killing yourself. If we get a free let the player who is fouled take it. Move it quick first time. Players will be loose. Frees: Seánie take them from the right. Tony, take them from the left and centre. If there is a penalty Tony you take it and drive it low and hard. Look lads, the team isn't finalised yet. We're going to sit down and have a look at it. If we change one or two so what? We have a lot of young players. You might not be picked today but you'll get your chance as the championship goes on. Work harder. The B team didn't play in Portlaoise but look at last Tuesday. There's no difference between the A and B team. There's only going to be one result. It's three weeks to round two and four to five weeks to the qualifiers. But we're not thinking about that. We're not going over to Portlaoise to be fodder for anyone. You're as good as anyone. One or two of you need to be a little bit fitter. Staff was in Australia and look at him now. Any one have any problems? If we do make a few changes to the team, so what?"

The manager then asks Leighton to say a few words. "Lads this is what we have trained for. Play your own game in your head.

Forget the qualifiers. We want Westmeath on the 14th. Let's give it one hundred per cent." Arthur urges the team to play the way they did last year against Kildare. "We have a full deck in Portlaoise. You're as good this year as last year." Jimmy Whittle tells the players to bring two sets of boots with them so they will have a choice.

The arrangements for Sunday are as follows: be at The Judges in Baltinglass at eleven o'clock We'll be departing for Portlaoise at 11.45 and as no one is interested in staying for the second game the post match meal will be at 3.45 in Portlaoise. The starting team will be announced in The Judges.

After the post training meal I am invited into the selectors' meeting where the final team selection will be made. The discussion goes as follows:

Arthur: Longford have a good first round record. They will be playing a physical game.

Micko: Sure that's what Glen Ryan is about.

Arthur: I think we should play Power at full-back. He's commanding over Seánie. One other change I'd make: Put Rory Nolan on instead of Jacko. Jacko isn't looking or playing well. On last night I'd prefer Darragh O'Sullivan to Dean Odlum. Dean hasn't played well in the championship. Yes, he has played well in the league.

Kevin: Power has been on Seánie who wasn't on song. Alan Byrne's man drifts out. Dean is getting more ball than anyone but he's not scoring. He's brave and wins ball. Darragh O'Sullivan isn't as brave and doesn't win as much ball.

Philip: We're picking a third on reputation only. We've started young lads in the past. This year, for example, Leighton, Paul Earls and Seánie haven't shown. Rory Nolan and Ciarán Doyle are on form. Too much on reputation: we need to pick the in-form players. Rory will give energy. I think we should consider using Rory instead of Jacko.

There is some discussion about the best position for Leighton

Glynn. He can be placed at half forward instead of half back. As a half back he sometimes attacks too much and is often caught out of position. There seems to be at least three areas of concern: the position of full-back and the half forwards and half backs. There is also a question mark over Seánie Furlong who is not in the best form of his life. But Seánie is still capable of turning a game around. After Paul Cunningham's exploits for the under twenty-ones, this player is suggested as a replacement for Dean Odlum or Darragh O'Sullivan. Perhaps Ciarán Jones could be considered too. If Paul Cunningham gets a bad start and is replaced what would the effect on his self confidence be? There is a growing consensus that Rory Nolan will start at wing forward as he is the player in form.

Another area of concern is the full-back line. On Tuesday's performance in training, Damian Power would be the first choice. The Rathnew man has a commanding presence and it is felt that perhaps Alan Byrne is not aggressive enough for the full-back position. Paul Barden, the Longford man who is expected to play full-forward is not considered to be the paciest of players. This would suit Damian Power. There are also question marks about Alan Byrne in the corner and the fact that Brian McGrath is not comfortable in the corner. Ciarán Doyle seems to be the in-form corner back of the moment. Another newcomer to the panel, Ciarán Jones has been showing up well in training. At the moment he is carrying a slight injury but he is expected to be fully fit within three weeks. And so the discussion goes on.

The final team selection is made but will not be announced until Sunday morning. It is: Mervyn Travers; Ciarán Hyland, Damian Power, Alan Byrne; Padge McWalter, Dara Ó hAnnaidh, Paddy Dalton; Thomas Walsh, James Stafford; Tony Hannon, Leighton Glynn, Rory Nolan; Dean Odlum, Seánie Furlong and Paul Earls. There will be joy for Damian Power and Rory Nolan and disappointment for Rory's brother Alan and 2008 Wicklow Footballer of the Year, Jacko Dalton.

SUNDAY 24TH MAY
Leinster Championship First Round, Portlaoise
Wicklow 2-12 Longford 1-13

The day is here. This is what the last six months have been about. This is championship day. The team assembles at The Judge's Inn Baltinglass at 11.00 for a light meal. Micko tells the players to go to the toilet and to come back and they'll have a little chat. The team is announced with the two changes.

Both Jacko and Alan are shocked. "Now look lads, there's no need for me to tell you the importance of today. This will be a tough one. They'll be fit. Challenge, tackle, harass. If you kick it wide, it's wide. Your first reaction should be: 'Where's my man?' Watch for the short kick outs today. When the ball goes out of play find your own man. Forwards tackle like demons. Paul Earls are you in good shape?" "I am Micko," replies the forward who is still studying in the UK.

"Backs, keep it tight. If Padge goes up the field Dara and Paddy Dalton stay back. James Stafford come back to the square to defend. When you get the ball your first reaction must be 'Who am I gonna give it to?' Their full backs aren't great. Paul Earls, we'll get word to you if we want you to come out. Half-forwards interchange. One thing that's most important, keep your mouths shut. For God's sake don't be talking to the referee. Play hard and tough but fair. When you tackle get the ball not the jersey. Keep your eyes on the ball at all times. We don't want to have anyone sent off. Tony Hannon, you take the penalties if we get any. Paul Earls has gone off form. (Much laughter.) Seánie take the frees from the centre. Lads, encourage one another. No giving out. Shout and encourage one another. One thing that's most important, don't be waiting for a free taker. If you're fouled get up like rockets and play the ball yourself. Quick and fast. Every bloody one of you can kick a free. For the first time we didn't know what to do with the team. It'll be very warm so we'll be sending on fresh legs. It's very important that we show a whole new united front."

At 11.50 a.m. the bus departs for Portlaoise. The mood in the bus is upbeat. There is a "Welcome Micko" flag on the bus. Kevin remarks: "We respect a good man when we get one." Peter Keogh is missing - the owner of The Judge's drives him to the bus. Andy O'Brien, chairman of the county board remarks: "If this was Ryanair we'd be gone."

When we arrive in Portlaoise the dressing room is very quiet. Some of the players are looking for new socks from Jimmy. Kevin is disappointed; he believes that a player should never wear new socks on a match day. In the dressing room is Bernadette O'Brien, the herbalist who has been supplying the team with natural energy drinks. The warm-up pitch is behind the county ground. It is quite a hot day so plenty of water is consumed. Back in the dressing-room the manager gives his final words of encouragement. "Look lads, it's just one hour and ten minutes. We want a hundred per cent commitment all the way through. Encourage one another. Watch the breaks. Move and think fast. Fight like tigers out there today with fire and brimstone. Prove it to the rest of the country that you're the best in Leinster."

Before the throw-in team captain Leighton Glynn goes around each of the team and encourages them. In the huddle he tells them: "You're as good as anything in Leinster. Prove it." Rory Nolan is given his first champion start. Power made two spectacular catches in the first half and Arthur enthuses: "Was that a good decision?"

Arthur is also the Maor Fóirne and Kevin who has been doing that job all through the league, is confined to the technical area. I sense that this is not to Kevin's liking. Kevin does a lot of the physical work with the team and often plays in the practice matches.

Longford bounced into a 0-3 to 0-1 advantage after 11 minutes as Glen Ryan's charges made a more settled start with Ger Dennigan (2) and Francis McGee on target. Tony

Hannon bagged Wicklow's four opening points as the Garden County took a 0-4 to 0-3 lead by the 19th minute - with all of Hannon's scores coming from placed balls. Wicklow continued to pile on pressure with Hannon kicking his side's first wide in the 22nd minute, while Dean Odlum's effort a minute later saw Wicklow break two points clear. However, Longford hit a purple patch with four points in as many minutes from Francis McGee (2), Brian Kavanagh and David Barden. That saw them take a 0-7 to 0-5 lead five minutes before the interval. But Wicklow took control at midfield once more and responded well with Earls cutting the deficit to a point at the break. *(Report from www.gaa.ie)*

At the break the selectors go into conference. Wicklow will have the advantage of the breeze this half and Leighton Glynn urges his team mates to keep it simple. Tony Hannon echoes this. "We'll tear them apart if we play, we haven't started to play yet. Remember this is the championship. This is the best chance Wicklow have had in six or seven years."

Thomas Walsh continues: "Look boys, stick with Barden for the kick outs. The next ten minutes are going to be the most important of the year. Seánie stay in the square and we'll deliver the ball." Ciarán Hyland stresses the importance of not giving an inch. "We've spent seven months preparing for the next thirty-five minutes. Don't give an inch. We're not playing well. We're ok, but we're only in second gear." Leighton continues: "Keep honest. Seánie will come into it when we give him the ball. Work rate. We're doing it but we're not doing enough."

Micko then comes into the changing room and says that they are going to make a few positional changes. Brian McGrath will move to centre back and Dara Ó hAnnaidh will go to full back. "Now lads, we're a little dead in our game. The wind won't do it for us in this half. We have to play quick and fast. Paul Earls stay up front. Inside forwards, stay inside your markers. Midfielders, don't over do the attacking. Keep it tight at the back. They're fast in the middle. We were caught out a few times with the kick outs. Alan Byrne how are you? Look lads, you have thirty-five minutes to stay in the championship. Go out there and die for Wicklow!"

Both sides hit purple patches on the restart, Wicklow's Championship debutant Rory Nolan slotting home an early goal with O'Dwyer's side holding a 7-point lead with 13 minutes remaining.

However, Longford weren't finished with a Padraig Berry goal bringing them back into contention. Still, Wicklow had the last laugh as Earls effort saw them advance to the next round. Earls and his colleagues made an explosive start to the second half as O'Dwyer's charges bagged an impressive 1-1 inside three minutes of the restart.

The Garden County drew first blood inside the opening minute when captain Leighton Glynn saw his shot come off the upright but the unmarked Nolan was well-placed to gather possession and slot the ball past Longford keeper Damian Sheridan.

Wicklow kept the momentum going with full-forward Seánie Furlong slotting over his first point as his side went 1-7 to 0-7 in front. Longford dominated possession over the next few minutes, but a resiliant Wicklow defence left Ryan's charges with no change with Kevin Mulligan and Barden both adding to Longford's wide count.

Wicklow continued to rack up points and built up a 1-11 to 0-7 lead with 12 minutes remaining but Longford were far from finished. Amazingly, and minus Kavanagh who had been substituted; Longford kicked 1-4 over a six-minute spell to level the contest for the first time in 36 minutes. Points from McGee and Kevin Smith, were followed by Berry's powerful 61st minute goal as points from Dennigan and Paul Barden drew the tie at 1-11 apiece.

But Earls led the late charge from the Garden soldiers, a more focused and determined Garden County side booking their passage to the last eight in the province. *(Report from www.gaa.ie)*

Back in the changing room the mood is fantastic. Rory Nolan is the star of the show and local radio and newspapers want to interview him. Micko congratulates the team and tells them that we now play Westmeath in three weeks time in Tullamore. "When we get over Westmeath we'll have the Dubs in Croke Park. There'll be training as usual in Aughrim on Tueday. Congratulations. Now don't get carried away celebrating."

Back in the hotel everyone is in great form. The owner of the hotel comes in and makes a short speech. He says that there is a tradition of making a presentation to the man of the match following a championship victory. On this occasion championship debutant Rory Nolan is presented with the man of the match watch. Peter Keogh then stands up and says a few words. "Yesterday I celebrated my 80th birthday. The chairman of the county board presented me with a silver watch and chair for which I am truly grateful. But you gave me the greatest birthday present of all today. Keep it up lads."

And so the Leinster adventure has begun. For two years in a row, Wicklow, the minnows of Leinster have won their opening match in the provincial championship. Let the journey continue.

TUESDAY 26TH MAY
Training in Aughrim

The sun is shining in Aughrim but it is not warm. The mood in the camp is good following Sunday's victory. Seánie Furlong is suffering from a dead leg and is unable to participate in the session. There is the usual warm-up lap followed by sprints. There are some ball passing drills with the emphasis on changing pace. There are some sit ups and press ups for which Kevin sets the pace. There are some hurdle drills. Micko addresses the players at the end of the session. "Now look lads, lack of concentration nearly lost us the match on Sunday. The backs were caught ball-watching. There are a few things we'll have to work at before the Westmeath game." With that the session ends.

THURSDAY 28TH MAY
Training in Aughrim

Today Cumann na mBunscol Cill Mhantáin hosted the Regional Festivals for the GAA/INTO Mini Sevens at the Bray Emmets GAA Grounds. One hundred children comprising of ten boys and ten girls from Wexford, Wicklow, Carlow, Kilkenny and Laois were trying to impress the assessors. Nine boys and nine girls, at least one from each of the five counties, will be selected to play in the exhibition matches at half time during the All Ireland semi-finals and finals. It is another beautiful day. Later on that night Cumann na mBunscol have their meeting to finalise arrangements for the county sports day. As I am attending that meeting I am unable to make Aughrim. I'm told that it was a good session. The previous night the junior team defeated Kilkenny in the Leinster championship. This was an opportunity for some of the fringe players to impress. Three nights in a row for some of the players and training again tomorrow night.

FRIDAY 29TH MAY
Training in Aughrim

Training begins with the usual warm-up run and some stretching. There follows some ball drills with the emphasis on picking up the pace. Micko calls the players together before the practice match. He emphasises the importance of holding the ball into the chest. Finally it is time for the practice match and the duel of the evening is Ciarán Hyland marking Leighton Glynn. The no hop no solo rule is applied and the maestro wants first time football all the way. There are some hard tackles put in but the hits are fair and no one is complaining. John McGrath is back running again and hopes to back to full time training in two weeks. The final part of the night's training consists of some sprinting back and forth across the pitch. Tony Hannon encourages his team mates: "This is where it is won and lost." Next up is a practice match late on Sunday afternoon in Newcastle.

SUNDAY 31ST MAY
Official opening of the newly-developed Newcastle Pitch

It's the Sunday of the June Bank Holiday weekend and is it hot. For the last few days the weather has been beautiful. Sunscreen is the order of the day – a far cry from the wintergreen of many a winter night's training session. Today there is a match between two Wicklow sides – the blues Wicklow, and the whites, Cill Mhantáin. Throw-in is not scheduled until 5.30 p.m. and it looks as if that might be optimistic. Players spoke to me about the lateness of the throw-in and how they were hanging around for a fair bit of the day knowing that they had a match to play. A mid-afternoon throw-in would have suited the players better. However this is a community day and there are various tournaments for adult and juvenile players. The newly developed pitch looks well and there is a sizeable crowd around. Kevin has brought his family along. This is typical of what the GAA is throughout the country – local communities coming together to celebrate our national games. And today the weather has looked favourably on the Garden County and its supporters.

Micko calls out the teams in the dressing room. Since the changing rooms are too small for both teams to be in one, the blue team is called out first and stay put. The white team go to the second dressing room. Both teams are given the same pre-match talk: Don't pick the ball off the ground. Armagh were caught out today. Refs are strict on picking up the ball. Keep your hands out when tackling and go for the ball with one hand. If you go to tackle with two hands you'll give away a free. Tackle the ball. Last Thursday at training in Aughrim there were some great scores – there was no hopping and no soloing and we got a huge number of scores. Quick and fast - that's the way Armagh and Tyrone play.

Peter Keogh climbed Lugnaquilla this morning and that might account for our octogenarian looking a little tired this evening. Nevertheless, Peter and county chairman, Andy O'Brien perform the honours at the official opening of Healy-Farrell Park. Eddie Farrell, after whom the pitch was being named died just the prevous Sunday. Ar dheis Dé go raibh a h-anam. There are the official team photographs before the game gets underway, but before this can happen there is a little banter between Damian Power and Padge McWalter. Both want to be captain today and insist on a toss of the coin to choose ends. After the official tossing of the coin both teams end up playing the way Micko said they would. Micko, once again is the referee.

It is a good competitive work-out with some of the fringe players showing decent levels of skill. Paul Cunningham, who is playing in the forward line for the whites scores two goals on Mervyn Travers, something that is not too easily accomplished. At half time the blues are trailing the whites on a score line of 3-6 to 1-10. Micko encourages his charges not to be using the F-word. "It doesn't look good and it sounds awful." He encourages them to say "flip" instead. Late into the second half there is a moment of concern when Thomas Walsh goes down and is attended to by Noel and Prem. He is replaced as a precautionary measure. The game ends and the players can go to the community centre for something to eat if they so wish. Micko tells them that in Kerry the players would go down to the sea and have a dip in the Atlantic Ocean on an evening like this after training. Somehow I cannot image the Wicklow players trudging down to the beach at Newcastle and getting into the Irish Sea. Micko tells them that it has been a good work-out and that there will be some lively sessions on Tuesday and Thursday, "with a little football".

Thus ends the month of May. It has been a good month for Wicklow – a victory in the championship and a quarter final meeting with Westmeath awaits. The panel, with the exception of John McGrath, is nearly at full strength. For the first time in the three years that Micko has been in charge there is plenty of talent on the substitutes' bench. This is good because no player can now be assured of his place based on reputation. From now on places will be given to players on how they have performed in training. May began with some sunshine in Aughrim and ended with glorious heat rays in Newcastle. Time to move up another gear.

CHAPTER SEVEN
Flaming June

JUNE began with a heat wave and temperatures during the first days of the month were higher than any recorded last year. The championship is really beginning to heat up too - Armagh have been consigned to the qualifiers along with the Cork hurlers. Of the eleven games played in the football championship so far this year, the Garden County is the only team to have beaten a team from a higher division. Hopes are high that this can be repeated on 14th June.

TUESDAY 2ND JUNE
Training in Aughrim

After two brutal summers it looks as if summer '09 is set to be the best since 2006. Hopefully it will be Wicklow's best Leinster campaign ever. Today temperatures of 26 degrees Celsius were recorded in Birr. As I arrive in Aughrim the team is already doing the warm-up laps. It is still very warm – what a contrast with wet and windy winter evenings in Knockananna. The panel does sprints of varying distances across the pitch - Micko at one sideline and Kevin O'Brien at the other. Have you ever noticed that we always refer to Wicklow's sole All star by both his Christian and surname? Yet Micko is simply Micko? The same Kevin is not a happy camper this evening. He feels that some of the players are not pushing themselves – some cannot train tonight because they are suffering from sun burn. This is the best opportunity that Wicklow have ever had – the County Board is fully behind the team and the team management and we have the greatest manager in GAA history ... yet some players still suffer from the malaise of

Wicklow where second best was always acceptable. One particular player is missing from training again and without any explanation. Kevin is becoming disillusioned with this attitude. He thinks of all the effort he has put in for his native county over the years and players still lack commitment. I wonder had he been born a few hundred yards further west would he have achieved more success with the Lilywhites? Micko calls in the players and says that last week and this week are hard sessions but next week there would be some tapering off ahead of the Westmeath game. Next week there would even be some "ground football. We don't play soccer!" There are thirty players so it's a game of fifteen-a-side without any hopping or soloing. Micko wants direct football "quick and fast".

I notice that the players are playing with much more intensity than I have seen to date. They have taken his advice about talking to each other. Both teams are very vocal with plenty of instructions being shouted at one another. Just before the final whistle Paddy Dalton shoulders his opponent who ends up on his backside wondering what has hit him! Micko tells the team on more than one occasion: "Right lads, this is the last kick-out. When he does actually blow for full-time one player asks if they can play on for a few more minutes.

Ahead of the warm-down Micko addresses the panel, "Look lads, one thing was proved tonight. Direct play works. Why? There is no need to hop and solo and ye took some marvellous scores. Why? Moving the ball upsets the backs. If you're soloing the back will get to you. We played first-time football in Kerry for twelve years and how many All Irelands did we win in that time? Look lads if you're 30 yards from the goal and there is a better-placed man inside give it to him or bang it over yourself. I want to see the right and left corner forwards inter-changing, and Seánie you come out and make space. That was a nice game of football tonight. The more you solo the more you'll be tackled. Quick and fast – that's the way we want you to play. Westmeath will probably have four forwards – we'll play our six backs, and James Stafford

I want you holding back and gathering the ball from our square. You're good at that. Well done lads and we'll see you all on Thursday night when we'll have another right good session."

Just before the team warms down Jimmy Whittle reminds them that on Friday the supporters and juvenile players will be coming along, so he wants all players in their navy training tops and white shorts. Jimmy Whittle: the man who wants to make Wicklow look like a unified team and kitted out to match the best in the country.

THURSDAY 4TH JUNE
Training in Aughrim

Micko drove up from Waterville this afternoon and will be going back tonight in order to vote in the local and European elections tomorrow. He will be travelling back up to Wicklow for tomorrow's training and home again tomorrow night.

Training tonight followed the usual pattern: a jog to warm-up, some sprinting, drills with the ball, and all of these are interspersed with stretching. The ladders are also in use this evening. Alan Byrne is having problems with his knee and he is resting it. There is the usual game of reds v yellows. I notice that tonight that the hits are harder and the tackling tougher. At the far end of the pitch Seán Kinsella pulls up. He is helped off the pitch and appears to be in some distress. It later transpires that he has torn his groin and it appears to be a bad tear too. Jacko Dalton leaves the pitch with a cut to his head. Tonight Dr. Cuddihy is attending training and repairs the cut. Jacko resumes his position in the game. The game is played at a ferocious pace and the hits are going in hard and often. No one is taking prisoners tonight. Thomas Walsh lands four hits. The recipients will know that they have been in a tough training session by the time tonight is over.

Following the final whistle Micko calls the panel together. These nights there is no problem with getting thirty fellows to train. He tells the assembled that the night's training was a little bit better.

"There were some great belts there and fellas kept on playing. That's what we want: more of that."

Micko tells the players that he had hoped to hold Sunday's training session on the pitch in Tullamore. When enquiries were made of the Offaly County Board Wicklow were told that they could, but that if it were wet that they would have to use another pitch. Micko was none too pleased with that and declined their offer. Training on Sunday will be in Aughrim as usual.

During the meal afterwards, Micko says that he'll have a little bit of poison – sure there's no harm in a little bit of poison (apple tart and ice cream) now and again. It transpires that Arthur likes ice-cream and following a match one year he stopped in every town and village between the venue and Baltinglass on the way home after the game. He even claims to have eaten three full blocks of ice-cream on one occasion. Watching how he was wolfing into the ice-cream this evening I would not be surprised if this were the truth, the whole truth and nothing but the truth.

FRIDAY 5TH JUNE
Training and Meet the Players Night in Aughrim

Today the local and European elections were held. I travel to Ballinrobe in Mayo to meet Bernadette O'Connor, the herbalist who has been providing some tonics for the panel.

When I meet Bernadette in her office she explains that she works on energy levels and tests clients for foods that they should avoid. She also uses magnet therapy. Following a lengthy consultation she recommends that I avoid wheat and any products that contain wheat. She also advises: "Don't touch the pig." She gives me some mixtures – two to be taken before meals and one to be taken after. She advises me not to touch the water in Wicklow unless it is filtered and to avoid any bottled water that has been filtered through limestone. French water and Kerry water are filtered through sandstone and are much better. She also advises that I take some supplements that are readily

The back room team get a taste for the sideline in O'Moore Park one week before the Longford game. Left to right: Martin Coleman, Martin Lott, Arthur French, Micko, Andy O'Brien, Philip McGillycuddy, Kevin O'Brien, Jimmy Whittle

Mervyn Travers shows why he is regarded as one of the best shot stoppers in the country

Damian Power and Padge McWalter watch as Micko tosses the coin

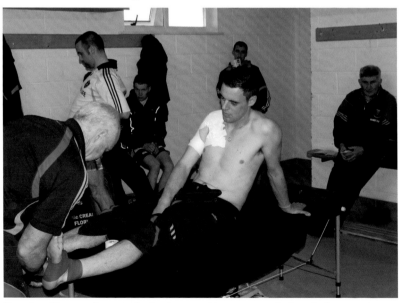

Damian Power shows why he is sometimes regarded as being Wicklow's Elastoplast Man

The selectors deliberate at half-time in Portlaoise during the practice match one week before the championship opener

Wicklow's man-of-the-match Rory Nolan being interviewed after the victory over Longford

Leighton Glynn signs a football flanked by Ciarán Hyland and Alan Byrne

Ciarán Jones (RIP) reads an article about Micko called 'A Timeless Classic' while the maestro is sitting in the seat directly in front!

Wicklow captain Leighton Glynn with ref Joe McQuillan and Westmeath skipper John Keane in O'Connor Park, Tullamore

Above: Alan Byrne falling awkwardly during the game, forcing him off for the rest of the game

Right: Paddy Dalton leaves the field in pain with a serious shoulder injury

Damian Power looks back towards the Wicklow goal and realises that three injuries to the Wicklow back line in such a short space of time is going to make the task very difficult

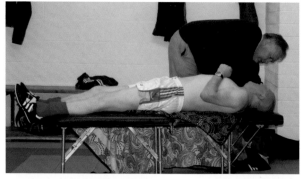

"I've seen better legs hanging out of a nest!" Paddy Kelly prepares Jimmy Whittle for the practice match ahead of the Fermanagh game

Above: Tony Hannon poses with a young fan following his Man of the Match performance against Down

Left: "Paul is ready for the Bahamas"

Micko shows how to relax before a vital championship game

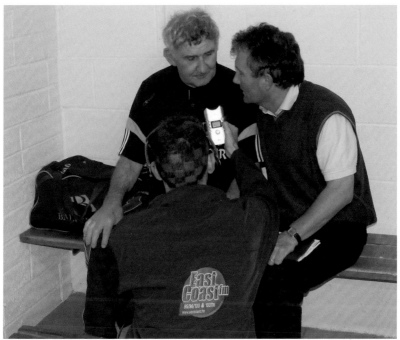

Gerry Grehan conducts an interview with Micko for East Coast FM

Over an hour after the final whistle Micko still has time to pose for photos and sign autographs

County Chairman Andy O'Brien shows his delight as Wicklow progress to the last twelve

Arthur talks about the Kildare draw to Newstalk while Micko looks on

available in the health shops. In particular she advises me to take green barley juice, which, if we are to believe the research, is a wonder food of nature. Alcohol should be avoided for three months, and lagers, ales and certain spirits that contain wheat should not be consumed. Stout is fine. Fruits to be avoided are those that contain citric acid such as oranges as research shows that these fruits can exacerbate the symptoms of arthritis. I do not suffer from arthritis but my mother does and on the law of averages I could be prone to the same, especially since I have run many marathons and have had some cartilage removed from my knee.

During my conversation with Bernadette I tell her that I believe that some of the panel were not taking the solutions because they did not like the taste of them. She is amazed at this. I tell her that sometimes it seems to me that training a county team is something akin to teaching primary school children.

Back in Aughrim it is a cool night. The players have attired themselves in accordance with Jimmy Whittle's wishes, but on account of the chill, some of them are also wearing long sleeved tops over their training top. Micko is pleased with the amount of work that has been done. He feels that the players are in exceptional shape. There is little over a week until the Westmeath game. Players are encouraged to keep their heads and to stay focused. They are told to shower, have their meal and then go upstairs to meet the children and their parents.

Upstairs in the large meeting room there is plenty of activity. The players are sitting along two rows of tables and the children are getting them to sign autograph books, match programmes and jerseys. Everyone from the administrator to the star players and selectors is called on to sign. Micko address the crowd before the players leave. He thanked the parents and the club officials who had brought the children along this evening. He added: "The children are the future of this county. We have a great bunch of players who will do well this summer. You have met the players and thanks for coming along. We'll see you all in Tullamore and then in Croke Park when we take on the Dubs."

SUNDAY 8TH JUNE
Training in Aughrim

Today Clare were defeated by Limerick in Munster SFC and Cork drew with Kerry in Killarney. Kerry missed a penalty and Cork were leading by five points late into the second half. But Kerry are not easily defeated and fought back and snatched an injury-time equalising point to set up a replay in Páirc Uí Chaoimh. In Croke Park Antrim's hurlers, playing in the Leinster Championship are beaten by Dublin. In the much-anticipated meeting of Dublin and Meath, the Dubs win by two points. Neither side performed particularly well with the winners notching up seventeen wides. If Wicklow were to defeat Westmeath next week there would be a day out in Croke Park against the Dubs on Sunday 28th June. The Dubs looked far from convincing.

TUESDAY 10TH JUNE
Training in Aughrim

It is a fine sunny evening. Training consists of the usual warm-ups and some sprinting. There is a period of kicking and then a practice match. The team for Westmeath has been selected but the players don't yet know it. Micko calls the players together and tells them: "That was a nice game. A good work-out lads. We'll play a little football on Thursday. The team goes to press tonight, but we'll be looking at you again on Thursday. We'll tell you what the starting team is on Sunday morning. Be prepared for changes. The juniors are playing Longford tomorrow in the Leinster semi-final. You have everything to play for. We'll rest for the remainder of this week. We need a tighter defence. Midfielders don't forget to defend and pack at the back. We'll see you all on Thursday."

THURSDAY 12TH JUNE
Training in Aughrim

It is a mild evening and there is a maximum turn-out for training. This is the usual pattern coming up to a championship tie – no one on the treatment table. Last night in Edgeworthstown the juniors were beaten by a point by Longford in the Leinster semi-final. Wicklow were in dire need of a reliable free-taker. Training tonight is very light. There is lots of kicking and then a warm-down lap. Micko calls the panel together.

"Now lads, I don't have to tell you the importance of Sunday. Win and we have a crack at the Dubs in Croke Park in front of 80,000 people. We beat Kildare last year in Croke Park. Kildare have the ambition to win Leinster this year. It's all about self-belief lads. Glennon will be the threat on Sunday. You must be ready to mark tight. Our six backs must play a defensive game. The Bomber always wanted the ball into his chest. Forwards stay out in front and win the ball. Half forwards and half backs pick up the breaks. We should win at midfield. Watch for the breaks between the two fifties. Flannagan is an attacking midfielder. Go for him. Run at him and he won't last. Play our game. Get the basics right. It will be great to play in Croke Park. You'll be as fresh as daisies on Sunday. Remember you're playing for a team. Where's the fisherman (Damian Power)? If you're going to be put off take Glennon with you! (much laughter). He's the only threat to our team. Ciarán Hyland, chase him around. The rest should be sorted out easily enough. My voice is gone because of all this shaggin' football, but you'll hear me on the sideline. Encourage each other. Don't give out and for God's sake keep your mouth shut. Don't open your mouth to the ref. He's a disaster. He had to be escorted off the pitch in Killarney two years ago. Quick and fast like the Kerrys and Tyrones. Arthur have you something to say?"

"Micko," I think you've covered it all," replies Arthur. Micko continues, "Whatever happens we're going to continue. We have the qualifiers this year, so we'll be training on Tuesday and Thursday.

It's about you, about Wicklow, about ourselves. Lads, you've worked hard. Don't let it go. There's a lot of hype about Wicklow. We have three weeks until the next round. Has anyone any questions?"

Padge McWalter has a concern about eating four hours before the game. Team captain Leighton Glynn says that not eating for four hours before a game is a long time, so there will be fruit on the bus. Padge says that the experts recommend eating two and a half to three hours before an event, to which someone adds: "Mammy will make your lunchbox." It's agreed to leave the breakfast until half past ten.

Arthur tells the players to use his herbal remedies if they feel unwell. No antibiotics. Arthur only uses natural extracts from plants - nothing from which the drug companies have made a fortune. Finally Leighton reminds his team-mates that they are in a Leinster quarter final. Glennon and Flannagan have been fighting. Do as we're asked and we'll be in a Leinster semi-final. We'll beat Westmeath because we are better and fitter.

SUNDAY 14TH JUNE
Leinster SFC Quarter-Final, O'Connor Park, Tullamore
Westmeath 0-16 Wicklow 1-10 (aet)

It is a warm and humid morning as the team assemble at The Judge's Inn in Baltinglass. There is a light breakfast of scrambled eggs and toast. Micko addresses the team. "Now lads, we're the underdogs today. There is no big pressure on anyone. I know we're going to win. There are no changes to the team. We've a good panel and we'll use it. Don't be hyped up. Treat it like another club game. What have Westmeath achieved? This is Division One against Division Four. Look lads, we're as good as anything in Leinster. We are on the road to success. In Laois it took a few years. Cork are building for six years now." (As Micko is speaking I look at Padge McWalter and I notice that he is hanging onto every word that the manager is saying. I notice another player and it seems that he is away with the fairies.)

"We're a better team. We're looking good all over the pitch. It's up to you lads. Look at where we'll be after this: Croke Park! Let them play their best team. (This was a reference to some of the more established Westmeath players coming back onto the panel.) Stay together. This is a game we must win. Enjoy the football. Let's bate the shite out of them."

The mood is upbeat on the bus. There is photograph being passed around the bus – one of Arthur with Bill Clinton. The joke is: Who is that man with Arthur? Micko retorts, "Put it away. Enough of that." From Stradbally there is a Garda escort to Tullamore. There are two motorcycles and a jeep. We make good progress and arrive in Tullamore at 12.40 p.m. The game will be shown live on television and there is a good atmosphere in the town. The sun is shining and the players are enjoying a kick around outside the changing rooms. RTÉ commentator Marty Morrissey comes into the dressing room and chats with Micko.

The team goes out onto the pitch for a look around. The warm-up takes place on the GAA pitch across the road from the county ground. As I go back to the changing room Jimmy Whittle asks me if I wouldn't mind going back to the training pitch and to look for Paul Earls' gum shield. As I go back to the training pitch I wonder if I am looking for a needle in a haystack. However I am lucky enough to be able to spot it fairly quickly and am able to deliver it to Paul before the throw-in.

Westmeath were two points ahead inside the first six minutes after debutant Conor Lynam had opened the scoring with a confident strike and Fergal Wilson tapped over a free after Dennis Glennon was fouled. However, Mick O'Dwyer's side had the ideal opportunity to haul their opponents back when they were awarded a penalty after Paul Earls, who was bearing down on an unguarded goal, was fouled by Francis Boyle, who was booked for a poor challenge. Tony Hannon stepped up to take the penalty, but his shot was straight at Gary Connaughton who batted the ball away to his right. Hannon, normally so reliable from placed balls, was struggling and he was guiltier than any other Wicklow player of adding to the seven wides they amassed in the first half. Incredibly, Wicklow had to wait for seventeen and a half minutes to get on the mark, Hannon knocking over a free after Dean Odlum was taken down. Four minutes later, Leighton Glynn, who burst through the Westmeath defence from centre-forward, scored their first point from play. Boyle, the Westmeath corner back, then found himself in unfamiliar territory and flicked the ball neatly over the bar to leave the Lake County two points to the good, 0-4 to 0-2. They looked to be in cruise control heading into the break with Hannon continuing to struggle for Wicklow. But Hannon found his range in the 31st minute and Odlum stole in for a fortuitous goal against the run of play to lead by two at the break. Thomas Walsh, the Carlow native, launched a high ball onto the square and Connaughton, the hero earlier with a fine penalty save, spilled the ball into the Wicklow man's path and he finished neatly from the ground to stun the O'Connor Park crowd. *(Report from www.gaa.ie)*

Jimmy Whittle speaks to the players as the selectors deliberate. "We have entered the war zone. Second place is not an option. We have put in seven months of training for today. Delete the first half. We're starting off the second half two points up. Play as if your life depends on it." Leighton adds, "Get into their faces. When we want to play we're brilliant. We can be like Tyrone. Their game is ten lads behind the ball. We play our game." Ciarán Hyland encourages his team mates to up the work rate. "Keep on hitting scores. We've two more gears. Give nothing away. Up the work rate. We'll walk off the pitch the happiest men in the world." Mervyn Travers adds that we have the better fitness on account of all the heavy winter training. Thomas Walsh chips in, "Boys, the breaks are vital. Dessie Dolan will come on. We had fear before the game. Not any more. We're good enough for a Leinster semi-final and a final."

When Micko comes into the dressing room he says that he cannot hear the team shouting and encouraging each other. "Keep possession if you've plenty of ground ahead of you. Let the ball go first time. We're being caught in possession. Quick and fast. Send in the ball intelligently. Our full forwards have the legs on the full backs. Tony? Calm down. Backs mark man for man. We're in a wonderful position. We have them on the run. Thirty-five minutes and we're in Croke Park. Rory I want to see more of you."

Odlum put Wicklow further ahead on the resumption of play before Westmeath hit five points in succession, Lynam and Glennon grabbing two apiece and David Duffy ending a fine spell of play with a point from midfield in the 52nd minute. The game was interrupted by a serious injury to Wicklow defender Alan Byrne, who suffered a suspected broken ankle. The Garden County ended a terrible spell when Seanie Furlong popped a short free to Hannon, who slotted the ball over the bar. Westmeath could have made the game safe in the 61st minute but Mervyn Travers, the Wicklow goalkeeper, made a good save from substitute Michael Ennis, who was set up brilliantly by Glennon. But it was O'Dwyer's men who found an equaliser, with James Stafford landing a fine point from play to level the game at 0-10 to 1-7 with five minutes left. Hannon looked to have won the game for Wicklow with a free in the final minute of normal time, but Lynam kicked his third point of the day and sent the game to extra time. *(Report from www.gaa.ie)*

Disaster struck Wicklow in the second half. Corner back Alan Byrne and wing back Paddy Dalton were both injured within moments of each other. Both have to leave the pitch with suspected broken collar bones. A few minutes later there is further bad news when full back Damian Power injured his ankle. Play continued and the ball went dead. The referee waves for play to continue despite Dr. Cuddihy's pleas that the player is badly injured with a suspected broken ankle. The referee does not stop play and in the absence of his marker the Westmeath full forward scores a point. At this stage the Westmeath team doctor assists Dr. Cuddihy and eventually Damian is stretchered off the pitch. The three Wicklow players are taken to Tullamore General Hospital. It later transpires that Paddy Dalton's collar bone is broken in two places; that Alan Byrne has torn ligaments in his shoulder, and that Damian Power's ankle might not be broken. Some time later it is confirmed that he has torn ankle ligaments. All three players will be out of action for six to eight weeks at least. Three backs gone is the space of five minutes but Wicklow refused to lie down. In the dying moments of the half Westmeath equalise and Padge McWalter receives his second yellow card and is sent off. He is distraught and apologises profusely to Micko who tries to console him as the players head towards the changing rooms. Because this is not a semi-final extra time will be played.

Leighton is on fire. "Subs will have to raise their game one hundred and fifteen percent. If a man has to come off we can send another man on. Surgery is the only reason why you'll come off." Thomas Walsh continues, "No one here is panting. We've plenty in the tank. They're shocked. What has Desie Dolan done? Hit hard boys." Micko comes in and is very animated. I have never seen Micko so animated. As he is encouraging the team he kicks a chair that is in the centre of the room. There is a cup on the chair and it falls to the ground and breaks.

In extra time there is further bad news for Wicklow. Paul Earls is injured and Paul Cunningham is prepared to enter the fray. At half time in extra time Westmeath are leading by just one point. Micko rallies the troops in the centre of the pitch. "We have it. The wind is with us. Play intelligent football. We have the legs on them. They're shagged."

Westmeath booked a Leinster SFC semi-final date with Dublin thanks to a three-point win over Wicklow at O'Connor Park, Tullamore on Sunday. However, it was far from easy for the Lake County, who needed extra-time to beat Mick O'Dwyer's side in a draining match that was interrupted by injuries and stoppages ... In the first period of additional time, Glennon and substitute Dessie Dolan nudged Tomás O Flatharta's men two points clear before JP Dalton left just one point between the sides at the break in extra time. However, the Lake County showed their class in the final ten minutes and when Lynam grabbed his fourth of the day from play, the game was up for Wicklow. Wilson added another free, his third of the game, to push his side further ahead before Darren Hayden reduced the arrears to just two with four minutes left. There was to be no late drama though and when Wilson added his fifth point of the game, Wicklow's dreams of a date with the Dubs in Croke Park was extinguished. *(Report from www.gaa.ie)*

In the changing room there is a deep silence. Micko tries to console the players. "There's no point in blaming ourselves. Had we won we wouldn't have been ready for the Dubs in two weeks with all the injuries. The championship is won with fire and guts. Are we hungry enough? Are we? We have to make things happen. We had plenty of chances. Look lads, forget about today. Over the seventy minutes we were the better side but we didn't take our scores. But look lads, we're not going down easily."

The bus journey to Portlaoise where there is the post match meal is rather subdued. What a contrast with the same hotel following the Longford match. Tony Hannon is silent. One can feel his pain and disappointment with his performance. Tony was the hero the last day. Today everything went against him. The Sunday Game is on the television in the function room. No one has the stomach to look at it. The final picture as the concluding credits roll is of Paddy Dalton as he is assisted from the field. As we board the bus big James Stafford is concerned about his club mate Damian Power. He is even more concerned about Damian's mother who will be a nervous wreck. He will ring her later on and try to reassure her that Damian will be alright.

Wicklow's assault on the 2009 Leinster championship is over for another year. Everyone knows that the team did not perform to their potential. The cynics in Wicklow will be on their hobby horse again – it seems that many Wicklow supporters prefer to gloat at the team's misfortunes rather than celebrate their successes. I wonder what Micko will do next? How can you pick a team up after a disappointment like that? Will Micko go after the qualifiers? These are questions for another day.

TUESDAY 16TH JUNE
Training in Aughrim

It is a cool evening in Aughrim. This is Bloomsday. The mood in the camp is mixed. On a positive note, John McGrath is back training having recovered from his broken collar bone. Micko says: "In Kerry many a player sat on the bench for a long time before going on to win All Irelands. On Sunday the ref didn't help. But our kicking is poor. Maurice Fitzgerald and all the great players spend time everyday kicking. Jesus lads, there are twenty-four hours in a day. Surely you could give one hour to kicking?"

THURSDAY 18TH JUNE
Training in Aughrim

It is a bright but cool evening in Aughrim. Brian Lennon, a man who has played for the team before has been recalled to the panel. Brian is a tall player who keeps a cool head when under pressure. He is a good addition to the panel. The Éire Óg players are missing tonight and there are just seventeen at training. Ciarán Walsh, has pulled out of the panel. Ciarán played in last year's campaign but has been dogged by injury this season.

Tonight there is a surprise 80th birthday party for Wicklow GAA President Peter Keogh. Peter is at training and poses for a few photographs with Prem who will be returning to India tomorrow to be with his wife who is about to give birth. Peter has been led to believe that Martin Coleman is bringing him along to a function to honour long-serving Wicklow Gael, Jimmy Dunne. Peter has even prepared a piece to deliver to the assembled in The Arklow Bay Hotel. As Peter took his place at the podium in front of three hundred invited guests, he was informed: "Peter Keogh, this is your life!"

Meanwhile back in Aughrim training consists of sprints of various distances, sit ups and press ups. Micko says that anyone who is defaulting on training should not be here. Word is being sent out to some promising minors to attend next week's training sessions. In particular, there is interest in St Pat's Tommy Kelly.

MONDAY 22ND JUNE
Training in Aughrim

It is a pleasant evening. I notice that there are only five of the starting fifteen from the Westmeath game participating in training. There are some on the treatment table, three with serious injuries while some are working.

In the practice match the no hop no solo rule applies. It seems that the team are rather lethargic, but as the game goes on more and more players increase their efforts. At the end of the game Micko calls the team together for a few words. "Lads, I have a question for you. Was it necessary to hop and solo the ball? That's how we're to play: give and go. For God's sake lads, don't be trying the impossible. There will always be players behind you. Don't be afraid to give it back. Don't be over holding the ball. Be more direct. Remember the basics. With a little extra effort we could have been facing the Dubs this Sunday. The back-up players are most important. That's what I can't understand about Wicklow. Someone comes to training for three or four nights and they think they can walk onto the team. Look at Ciarán Walsh. He wasn't getting his game so he walked away. Look at Ógie' Moran's son or any number of Kerry players. They'll sit on the subs' bench for years before they'll get their chance. Wicklow fellas sulk if they're not on the team. Wearing a county jersey is a tremendous honour regardless of the number. There's no need for more training now. From now on it's more football. One more thing that's most important lads, give the ball and run. There's nothing worse than giving it and standing." And with these words the first of this week's training comes to an end.

WEDNESDAY 24TH JUNE
Training in Aughrim
This is a great spell of sunny weather. The latest news is that Ciarán Hyland has been drawn to play in the National Lottery's Big Money Game at the weekend. There are twenty-two training tonight - sprints and a practice match. During the sprints Rory Nolan pulls up as a precaution. Is there a problem with the hamstring? Micko cautions the players at the end of the session - no fooling around or messing. No stepping out of line. No taking a drink. Get rid of the last day. We'll take a little look at the video of the Westmeath game next week and see the mistakes we made. The less we hop and solo the fewer mistakes we make."

FRIDAY 26TH JUNE
Training in Aughrim
Kevin O'Brien is at a graveyard Mass as is unable to attend training. There is a gentle warm-up followed by the practice match. The big surprise in the practice match is that reserve goalkeeper Billy Norman is playing in midfield. Staff and Walshie look out. Jimmy Whittle is playing in goal for one of the teams,

although a cynic might say that he is standing there. The manager is concerned about the Wicklow obsession to bounce the ball as soon as a player gets it. Dr. Cuddihy joins the team for the post match meal. Micko refers to the three injuries sustained against Westmeath and jokes to the good doctor, "You didn't stop breaking them up until you got a Greystones man on the team!" Micko leaves after the meal to drive home for a wedding in Killarney the following day. He'll be back on Sunday for training.

SATURDAY 27TH JUNE
RTÉ studios
Ciarán Hyland wins €124,000 on the National Lottery's The Big Money Game. During the games Ciarán chose the number two. When asked by the host of the show, Derek Mooney, why he did, the defender replied that it was his lucky number and also his jersey number. In two of the three games it didn't bring him much luck but he did win a substantial prize in the big money game. Hopefully he'll be seeing more success next Saturday against Fermanagh whom Wicklow drew in the qualifiers.

If Wicklow had played to their potential and beaten Westmeath, they would be facing the Dubs in Croke Park tomorrow. Kildare who were knocked out of Leinster last year by Wicklow defeated Laois tonight. It was Laois who narrowly defeated us last year in the Leinster Championship. Wicklow cannot too far away from the big breakthrough.

SUNDAY 28TH JUNE
Training in Aughrim
It is a fine morning in Aughrim. Word is coming through of a terrible tragedy. Ciarán Shannon, a former Wicklow player who still plays with his club Annacurra, died in a road accident yesterday. Ciarán was driving to Blessington to play a club match. In the car with him were his three daughters and his five month's pregnant wife. Travelling northwards along the N81 close to the

junction for Hollywood an oncoming car collided with the Shannons' car. Ciarán died at the scene but the rest of his family escaped any serious physical injury. Team mates of Ciarán who were travelling behind rendered assistance to all of the injured, but tracically there was nothing that could be done for their friend.

On a much happier note, another Ciarán, that is Ciarán Hyland, is at training and is being congratulated. Typical of the man he is modest in the extreme about his good fortune. The road tragedy however has everyone feeling sadness and loss.

Micko calls the players together after the match. "Kildare were beaten by us last year. That is the best thing that happened to them. They have been training five and six nights a week ever since. Lads are training on their own. That's the way it was when I was with them and they won two Leinster titles and played in an All Ireland final. We're as good as Kildare and Kildare are in the Leinster Final this year. For God's sake lads, we must up the work rate. What you're doing is ok for club level, but this is a different level. Another big effort. We have Fermanagh here next Saturday. Train hard. If we can get over Fermanagh anything is possible. Bang it over the bar if you have a chance. No soloing. First time football and get the ball into the forwards quick and fast. You're in good shape. We'd like you in better shape, but we can do no more with you. Look at the man with 110 cows (Stephen Fanning). He was going for a ball and James Stafford hit him. Look at the plaster on his forehead."

Later on in Croke Park Dublin destroy Westmeath by twenty-six points to qualify for their fifth successive Leinster Final. All I can think is that if it had been Wicklow playing the Dubs in Croke Park it would have been a much tighter affair.

TUESDAY 30TH JUNE
Training in Aughrim
It was a very hot day and the last of the primary schools in the

country got their holidays today. Earlier in the evening I was speaking to the parish priest of Annacurra. The funeral of Ciarán Shannon had been held that morning. Fr. Hammell said that it was the biggest funeral that had ever been in Annacurra. The night before Ciarán's team mates carried the coffin from the main Aughrim road to the church. The local community did a huge clean-up of the village and sandwiches and refreshments were prepared. Footballers from Sligo with whom Ciarán had played while studying there had travelled to attend the funeral and formed a guard of honour. Despite the brilliant sunshine this had to have been one of the saddest days of the year in Wicklow football. Only last week Tom Honan died while attending a match, and a few weeks before that Fr. Tom passed away. Alan Byrne, still nursing his injured shoulder and a team mate of Ciarán Shannon looks a bit shook after the events of the last few days.

Paddy Dalton, has his arm in a sling. His collar bone is broken in two places, but he cannot resist the temptation to kick a few balls. After the training session which consisted of some physical work and a practice match Micko called the team together. He singled out Paul Earls to illustrate a point about the risk of losing the ball in a tackle if you hop it. Paul had an opportunity to have a shot at goal against Westmeath but he hopped the ball and the backs cleared it. Paul's instant reply was: "I thought I was out of steps Micko," to which someone quipped: "He's spent he last two weeks thinking up that excuse."

Six months on in this journey and I wonder if I am nearing the end of the road. If we could just get over Fermanagh ....

CHAPTER EIGHT

Last Chance Saloon

IT'S make or break for Wicklow this month - in fact within four days of the beginning of July the team will either be looking forward to round two of the qualifiers or the inter county scene will be over until 2010. The result against Fermanagh on Saturday will determine the rest of the season.

THURSDAY 2ND JULY
Training in Aughrim

There was fairly heavy rain for most of today. Towards evening the rain stopped and there was heaviness in the air. Arthur is not togging out tonight. Jimmy Whittle is having some treatment from Paddy Kelly. The banter is that he is looking to get into the team for the Fermanagh game. Rory Nolan who is sitting out training tonight responds immediately: "I've seen better legs hanging out of a nest!" Time to go outside and do some kicking. Outside on the pitch there is some kicking practice -nothing too strenuous. Micko then calls the team together to give some encouragement and advice. The first instruction is that the players are not to talk to the referee under any circumstances. Against Westmeath on at least four occasions the referee moved the ball forward because someone said something. The manager then added that we would be using more men. "There will be no pressure on any player. We're the underdogs. It's crazy getting tense before a game. Do your best. No one is going to shoot you. This isn't South America."

Micko then spoke directly to Tony Hannon. Tony, who couldn't do anything wrong in the Longford game had a nightmare against Westmeath. Having the penalty saved early in the game seemed to have shaken his confidence and he never recovered. "Tony Hannon, you're a little bit tight. I'll shake you like I did in the game against Tipp," to which there is much laughter and the tension is broken. The maestro continues: "For God's sake don't be trying to shoot from impossible angles. If you're right-footed don't be trying to shoot from the wrong side. Stop, turn and curl it over. We should have beaten Westmeath. We lost three backs in a very short space of time and then we lost Padge. Look lads, we're there or thereabouts. We'll win if we play the ball quick and fast."

Micko then named the team: "In goal Mervyn Travers, full backs: Ciarán Hyland, Darragh Ó hAnnaidh, Stephen "Chester" Kelly, half backs: Padge McWalter, Brian McGrath, Darren Hayden; midfield: Thomas Walsh and James Stafford; half forwards: Leighton Glynn, Tony Hannon, JP Dalton; full forwards: Dean Odlum, Seánie Furlong and Paul Earls. Now look lads, we'll be bringing on subs. If you come off don't be getting thick. Wish the sub well. We'd love to draw Kerry in the next round. You're bloody good enough. Now we'll go inside and show you some mistakes."

Speaking quietly to me Kevin O'Brien said that he was feeling "like a spare tool" at this stage. It was now up to the players on the pitch. They can sweat it out on the pitch. All we can do is shout. It's up to them now. I hope this isn't the last supper." Kevin then told me that earlier in the day Arthur and Micko had rung Alan Byrne from Annacurra and arranged for the injured player to bring them over to visit Mrs. Shannon and the family where they offered their sympathies. Within six days towards the end of June Wicklow GAA lost two great Gaels. The driver of the other car in the accident that claimed the life of Ciarán Shannon died earlier today. Ar dheis Dé go raibh a h-anam.

SATURDAY 4TH JULY
First Round of the Qualifiers, Aughrim
Wicklow 0-17 Fermanagh 1-11

The match is scheduled to begin at 7.00 p.m. Tonight I will be Maor Uisce a Dó and I am looking forward to the role. For most of the day I found that I could not settle to do anything at all. It seemed as if the hands of the clock were standing still.

The panel was told to assemble in Aughrim at 5.45 p.m. but by the time the late afternoon had come I'd decided that I couldn't wait any longer and I had to leave for Aughrim. I arrived in Aughrim about 5.15 p.m. Noel Molloy had already set up and Jimmy was togged out. He gave me my official Maor Uisce 2 top and I changed into it. Martin Lott told me that he was unable to settle down to anything either during the day and that he couldn't wait for the game to start. Players began to arrive and Micko, upon his arrival made his usual comment: "And how are you feeling Martin (Coleman)?"

There had been some heavy showers during the day but these had now stopped. A worry is the whereabouts of Ciarán Hyland but he shows up in time to complete a warm-up. In the changing room the jerseys are given out. There is only one change to the published team: Leighton and Jacko are to swop wings. Micko gives his last bit of advice: "Two half backs stay back at all times. We have plenty of forwards. Midfielders don't forget to defend. Thomas Walsh, you know exactly what to do. One pick up could probably decide a tight game. I want ye all to go for this with body and soul. Dive in with life and limb. We want total commitment from you. We don't want this 'Will I or won't I go for that ball?' Go out there and give it everything."

Before the match began there was a minute's silence in memory of three Wicklow Gaels who had did recently; Fr. Tom, Tom Honan and Ciarán Shannon. During the silent tribute to these men I found myself with the rest of the mentors standing shoulder to shoulder with the team. For the first time in my life I experienced what it is like to be on the pitch just minutes before a crucial championship tie. The more I think about it the more this journey of mine has been a journey of self-discovery. I rigidly stuck to the instruction that the second maor uisce was to stay on the far sideline. I did notice that the two water carriers from Fermanagh were running onto the pitch at every break in play. After about ten minutes I felt that I was surplus to requirements. I had left eight half litre bottles of water along the sideline, but none of the players was taking any. At a break in play I asked the linesman if it were ok to go onto the pitch. He said that as long as there was a break in play that that was fine. I asked would I be the cause of a fine because I was the second water carrier and he replied that he didn't think so unless they changed the rules again.

And so began my forays onto the pitch. Players from both sides drank readily from the bottles. Coming close to half time the linesman told me to have a word with James Stafford. Staff was already on a yellow card and had spoken a few times to the referee. If Staff persisted with this he too would be joining Tony Hannon on the sideline. Going off the pitch at half time I told Martin Coleman what the linesman had said and he passed on the message to Micko.

In the changing room Jimmy Whittle spoke quietly. "This is the loudest silence we could ever have." Tony Hannon is sitting a dejected figure forlorn and alone in the corner. One or two of the lads go over to him to offer him some moral support, but in a moment like this a player has to face his own demons and nothing that anyone can say will make it otherwise.

Thomas Walsh speaks to the team. A leader is needed now and Walshie is not afraid to step up to the mark. "We've all been involved in matches with a man down. We have to work harder. This northern team thought that this would be a stroll in the park. Get the ball in fast to Seánie." Ciarán Hyland speaks about Micko. "Don't let this be Micko's last game after three years.

Micko enters the dressing room. He says quite calmly: "We're a better team." With that he went over to James Stafford and spoke quietly to him (shut up mouthing off or you'll be put off). There is a positional change to compensate for the missing Tony Hannon. Paul Earls will join Leighton and Jacko in the half forward line. Dean Odlum and Seánie Furlong will stay in the full forward line.

"Look lads, don't be over anxious. Teams down a man often play better. That last score was fabulous. We didn't hop the ball once. For God's sake watch the yellows. Go out there and win it for Wicklow."

For me the second half was both the longest and shortest thirty-five minutes in my experiences with the team. As the pace increased I found myself running onto the pitch more and more frequently. By the time the final whistle sounded I was hoarse and bathed in sweat. I felt as if I had run as much as any of the players on the pitch. What an experience of euphoria after the final whistle. I never experienced such unbridled joy and exhilaration. If the feeling of achievement could be bottled and sold there would be a world cure for depression. For the first time this year it seemed as if the cynics and critics of Wicklow football had been silenced. This was by far the team's greatest hour - they did all their talking on the pitch. With two men down they did exactly as Micko had said. They put their bodies on the line and took the hits and knocks, got up and said nothing to the referee. Knowledgeable sources would later say that this was Wicklow's finest hour since 1986 when they knocked Laois, the then National Football League Champions, out of the Leinster Championship.

Wicklow overcame the dismissals of Tony Hannon and Thomas Walsh to record a shock win over Fermanagh at Aughrim. Mick O'Dwyer's side went into the game without half of their regular defence, but they made light of the situation to record a stunning and surprising win. A James Sherry goal had seen the Erne men go in 1-5 to 0-7 up at the break and the Garden County looked in deep trouble after free-taker Hannon had been sent off for a second yellow card offence. However, with Paul Earls and Seanie Furlong to the fore, the home side scored a famous win with a powerful second half performance. *(Report from www.gaa.ie)*

At the post match meal afterwards in Lawless' Hotel, there were plenty of sore bodies but smiling faces. Amongst the mentors there was the feeling of a job well done and everyone was basking in the satisfaction that brings. Wicklow didn't make one substitution during the game. Championship debutants, Darren Hayden, Chester Kelly and Brian McGrath played out of their skins. Asked why he didn't make any changes Micko said that he was often accused of not changing a team that was winning. His reason? Why change the team if it is winning?

SUNDAY 5TH JULY
Training in Aughrim

It is a damp morning but spirits are really high after yesterday's win over Fermanagh. Micko is talking to the players who are gathered in a circle around him. He tells them that they have years of football ahead of them and he cannot understand players who walk away from the panel because they are not on the first team yet. "Look at what happened against Westmeath: three fellas got injured and three more got their chance yesterday. Put in the work and you'll get there. There are many fine hurlers in Kilkenny who can't get on the team but they persevere. Their time will come." With that he divides the players into two groups – those who were playing last night are to have a kick around – nothing too strenuous after their exertions against Fermanagh. The rest will do some physical work with Micko and Kevin. I notice that there are only about six of the team for the kickabout, but as the morning wears on most of them show up. Seánie Furlong and Paul Earls are not taking part in the session.

Training consists of sprints of various lengths and stretching exercises. There is a heavy shower and a clap of thunder, but luckily the rain passes over.

Micko advises the players: "Perseverance is the most important thing in life. Maybe last week you drank ten pints. This week you might drink two and next week you won't drink any. You might even cut it out altogether. I never drank and it did me no harm. I travelled the world playing football and I never took a drink. Other players would be on the beer. The next morning I would always feel great while the rest were looking for a cure. That was a marvellous display last night. But don't get carried away with it. A pitch is a pitch wherever it is. Keep it up. A few years ago in Kildare we were playing a Leinster championship match against Laois and we had two players sent off in the first half. Kildare took the game by the scruff of the neck and won. Kildare became a force that day. They went on to win two Leinster titles and appeared in an All Ireland final. Everyone from number one to thirty-two has to put in the work. Everyone matters. Tuesday and Thursday night again and another match on Saturday: maybe we'll even get Kerry here."

The draw for the next round of the qualifiers was made. Wicklow were drawn against Cavan and it later transpires that it is a home venue again for us.

TUESDAY 7TH JULY
Training in Aughrim

It is a dull evening in Aughrim but there is a good turn-out for training. Seánie Furlong and Dean Odlum are not taking part in training tonight - still feeling the effects from Saturday. After the first round of the championship there was much praise lavished on the team for the performance against Longford, but the next round of the championship was, what some might say, one of our worst performances ever. Cavan are a side that can be beaten but they did knock Fermanagh out of the Ulster championship. However, Cavan, in turn, were knocked out by Antrim who are now in the Ulster final.

Micko called the players together at the end of the session for a few words of encouragement. He advised them not to believe whatever was being written in the papers. In last Saturday's papers Wicklow were incapable of winning anything. Twenty-four hours later they were being mentioned as potential All Ireland champions - and this from the same journalist. "What won the game for us yesterday was fire, heart and passion and everyone playing for each other. There was no pulling out of tackles. If we repeat that passionate performance we will beat Cavan. It is now time to forget about Fermanagh. That game is over and all our energy will now go to concentrating on beating Cavan."

THURSDAY 9TH JULY
Training in Aughrim

By the time training began the sun had come out and the pitch in Aughrim was looking splendid. During the kick about Micko was hit on the head with a ball and was stunned for a couple of seconds, but thankfully he was uninjured. It was a light training session with plenty of kicking back and forth across the pitch.

Micko called the lads together and had a chat with them. He said, "You know exactly what you have to do. Tommy Carr is a good manager and will have Cavan well prepared. Don't underestimate them. We're getting too many yellows. No rugby-type tackling. That kind of thing is a yellow card straight away. Discipline is most important. If you speak to the ref he will move the ball up fourteen yards. Keep your mouths shut. That's most important. Play hard but fair. Encourage one another. Our goalie is great at shouting and roaring. Mervyn can see everything. Listen to him. Cavan will be breaking the ball down. They are weak at midfield and up at the front. I just got the tape of Cavan's game and I'll take a look at it. I'll tell you who kicks with the left or right. It's most important that you know which foot your opponent kicks with. Ciarán Hyland you'll be busy marking your man on Saturday. Look lads, you're in good shape. Play with fire and spirit and we can beat Cavan and go further. Paul Earls, where are you?"

"I'm here Micko."

"Paul, we'll keep you inside and we'll bring you out. Darren Hayden, keep an eye on your player. Chester, great to see you play so well."

Jimmy Whittle said that we'd be wearing the white jerseys. We had lost the toss but that was all we were going to lose: white jerseys and blue nicks. "Wear your navy gear travelling to Aughrim. We are an army travelling together. The forecast is for rain so make sure you have your two sets of boots and have your own gloves."

At the meal there was a tape of the Fermanagh game playing. There was much silence as each and every one of the players savoured the victory. At the end there was a clip that showed each of Wicklow's 17 scores. Just before the panel dispersed Arthur French spoke to the players. He said that there was a minute's silence before the game last Saturday in memory of Fr. Tom. The team was foremost in his mind right up until his death. During what turned out to be Arthur's final visit, of the team, Fr. Tom said: "When I go upstairs I'll be able to help more."

Fr. Tom, Arthur believed, was a saint and encouraged the players to call on him in their own personal lives. Arthur believed that it was Fr. Tom's spirit that helped us on our way to victory last Saturday. There was a minute's silence and then the players dispersed.

SATURDAY 10TH JULY
Second Round of the Qualifiers, Aughrim
Wicklow 1-12 Cavan 0-8

By early afternoon the dark clouds had begun to gather and by four o'clock the rain had begun to fall. In Wexford Park the home county drew with Roscommon after extra time in their qualifier. Sligo beat Tipperary and Kerry had taken a substantial lead over Longford early in their match. In the end the Kingdom just beat their opponents by four points and went for nearly half an hour in the game without scoring. Kieran Donaghy was assisted off the pitch with a suspected broken bone in his foot. This was later confirmed and 'Star' will be out of action for at least six to eight weeks. I arrived in Aughrim just before half five and I was surprised at the number of cars already in the car park. By now the rain was teeming down and I suspect the early arrivals wanted to be guaranteed the shelter of the stand.

When I went into the changing room there was a strange atmosphere, quiet but different to the quiet of concentration. Conversation was also strangely muted. Noel was working alone – the second physio had not shown up. The team went through their warm-up routine out on the pitch. Half an hour before the throw-in there was quite a crowd present. Once again I was honoured to be Maor Uisce a Dó so I would be seeing the game from the sideline adjacent to the stand. Philip MacGillicuddy had to tell me to turn my bib around – being nervous before the game I had put it on back-to-front.

At 6.35 p.m. Micko gave his final talk to the team. "Now look lads, I don't want anyone to be anxious about today. I don't have to preach and roar at you. What happened against Fermanagh the last day is of no consequence today. Half backs, it's most important that you don't over attack. Now look lads, I don't want anyone talking to the referee. Think back to last week. Did the referee change his mind? Even once? Just get on with the game. Penalties and frees have been covered. Watch for the short kick outs – that's most important. For God's sake lads, don't be picking the ball up off the ground! They've a deadly free-taker. Midfielders I want you to clean up everything between the two fifties. No jersey pulling! Don't be giving away simple frees. We want to go another step. NOW GET OUT THERE AND DIE FOR WICKLOW!"

Despite the heavy rain the game is played in a good spirit. Wicklow contest every ball and after the initial opening minutes begin to set the pace. Paul Earls beats James Reilly in the Cavan goal to a high ball and the green flag is raised. Going in at half time, Wicklow are leading 1-6 to 0-5. Many of the players are changing their socks. Some are wringing out their gloves such is the amount of rain that has fallen. Padge McWalter is having another superb game and reminds the team of the need to keep up the work rate. "We had a good lead and we dropped off and they came back at us. We need to up our work rate again. We worked hard last week when everything was against us." Leighton Glynn who is also playing a leader's role encourages: "First things first. Get that ball into your chest. They'll foul you. The ref won't let it go in case there are any pile ups. We're in control. We tailed off because we stopped playing our game. Seánie and the boys are lethal inside." Thomas Walsh reminds his teammates that Cavan's whole game plan is centred around Seánie Johnson. "If Staff or me are going forward the rest of you stay back. They'll be looking for Johnson. We'll be back. Simple football boys." Full back Dara Ó hAnnaidh who is growing more and more confident in his number three role warns them about mouthing off to the referee.

Micko then came into the room. He speaks quietly: "We don't want to lose this lead. We've lost leads in the league on this pitch. Their full back line is not coping well. Get the ball in quick and fast. Keep the ball moving. Backs don't over attack. Little things make a difference. Play for one another. Don't let it slip. Stand up now. Now lads, all of you on yellows be careful. No high tackles and no rugby tackles. Thirty-five minutes to die for Wicklow"

And what a thirty-five minutes it proved to be! The spectators were treated to probably the best performance seen in years in Aughrim. The history books show that the last time that Wicklow won two championship matches back-to-back was in 1986. That statistic was re-written today. Despite the torrential rain the team played exhibition football for the remainder of the half. Cavan only managed three more points to Wicklow's six. The mood in the changing room afterwards was electrifying. Fans mingled with team mentors and players. Micko gave numerous interviews after the game, both to the local and national media. He told the team that they could have a day off from training tomorrow and that they could go to the leisure centre in the Arklow Bay Hotel for a swim if they liked. He encouraged them not to go mad on the beer and that we would have training on Tuesday and Thursday nights and hopefully another home match next Saturday.

Wicklow's brilliant run in the 2009 GAA All Ireland Championship shows no signs of halting after Mick O'Dwyer's side pulled off a 1-12 to 0-8 win over Cavan in Aughrim on Saturday night. In a game played in atrocious conditions, the Garden County got the only goal of the game when Paul Earls punched to the back of the net after good work by Leighton Glynn. Wicklow led by 1-6 to 0-5 at half-time. Tony Hannon, who had a superb game, and Darren Hayden pushed Wicklow further ahead after the break, but Larry Reilly and Seánie Johnston hit back for Cavan. However, the Breffni comeback never really materialised and it was Wicklow who finished the stronger. (Report from www.gaa.ie)

SUNDAY 12TH JULY

No training today. This is the first Sunday since I began this journey last January that I haven't had to attend a training session or a match. In the Leinster Final Dublin defeat Kildare 2-15 to 0-18 in what many declared to have been the best match of the championship so far this year. This was also Dublin's fifth title in a row. In the draw for the next round of the qualifiers Wicklow will be at home to Down. This match will also be televised live with a three o'clock throw in.

TUESDAY 14TH JULY
Training in Aughrim
It is a damp evening in Aughrim following a day of heavy showers. The pitch is in great condition, a tribute to Victor Shaughnessy

and his pitch development committee. Training begins and it seems to me that some of the players are lethargic and not fully focused on the task in hand. I suspect that some of them may have been celebrating following the victory over Cavan. All I hope is that they have gotten it out of their system and are now ready to surmount the next challenge. It is good to see Alan Byrne taking part in the warm ups, but he knows himself that he is not yet ready to participate in the games. Rory Nolan does some running but his hamstring has not yet fully recovered. Paddy Dalton is without his sling. He is doing some light running but knows that his injury has him sidelined for the foreseeable future. A worry is seeing Brian McGrath limp off the pitch during the practice match. Hopefully it is just a precaution.

After the match Micko addresses the assembled players: "Now lads, you know exactly what's ahead. It's amazing lads that we've played two hard matches and haven't used any subs. We're sorry about that but I'm always reluctant to change a winning team. Hang in there. There are bound to be injuries when we have along run in the championship. Keep smiling. And why are we playing so well? Because we're playing as a team. We're not selfish. We're letting the ball go quickly. We're getting the basics right. If we get over this we're looking at a quarter final. But look lads, we're looking no further than Down. People are saying it's because we're playing in Aughrim. That's rubbish! Aughrim is a football pitch. Last year we beat Kildare in Croke Park. We're not getting injured because we're fit. There will be O'Byrne Cup matches in January. We've a great bunch of young lads here. Be positive. Is there anything as good as the feeling from the last two days? We're gonna keep it going. We do all the heavy work in winter. It's football in summer. We know exactly what we have to do: penalties and frees? This will be our fifth game in the championship. Sure I won an All Ireland with Kerry after playing just four matches. We're not gonna stop winning because we're enjoying it. Ok lads, we'll see you all here on Thursday night."

Copies of the latest issue of Garden GAA are available and James Stafford features on the cover. He is showing his delight after the final whistle in the Fermanagh match. He thinks I am responsible for that photograph, but unfortunately I cannot take the credit for it.

THURSDAY 16TH JULY
Training in Aughrim

Photographer Dave Barrett is taking head and shoulder photographs of the players in advance of Saturday's televised third round qualifier against Down. Tonight training is very light. After a warm up and some stretching there is some kicking from side to side across the pitch. At the end of this Micko calls the panel together and goes over how he wants the different lines to play.

"There's great work going on throughout the field. Tony Hannon - it's great to see you back to your best. Now look lads, these fellas are no giant-killers. The days of the guys from the north coming down here and beating us off the pitch are over. We've sussed out their defensive game. Now look lads, there's no need for me to tell you that this is going to be a hard one. We've had five games in six weeks. Don't be selfish. If there's a better-placed man give it to him. These are the little basics. We've covered the frees. The same as the last day. Padge McWalter? We haven't had any penalties but you'll take them if we do. Now lads, this game is on television. Isn't it great! There'll be more television if we get over this one. The prize is a quarter final in Croke Park. Look lads, it's only another game of football. There's no pressure on you. Play for yourselves above all and then for the county. We want you to enjoy this. And we want more enjoyment. Look lads, you're as good as any group I had in Kerry. When I came here what I wanted from you was fire and brimstone. We have it now. Arthur have you anything to add?

"Nothing, Micko. Not even Charles Steward Parnell could follow that!"

"Kevin?"

"Nothing to say Micko."

"Right lads, you know I think there could be an All Ireland in this team yet! Off you go and we'll see you all on Saturday at a quarter to two."

Another training session ends. There is no great excitement, yet one feels that the players are totally focused on what they have to do and for the first time a Wicklow team believes that it can go further than any Wicklow team has ever gone. Parting words to Eddie the chef from everyone are: "We'll see you on Tuesday." Bomber Liston and Joe Brolly, both speaking this week to Des Cahill on Drivetime Sport believe that Wicklow will do it.

SATURDAY 18TH JULY
Third Round of the Qualifiers, Aughrim
Wicklow 1-15 Down 0-17

Unlike the previous two Saturdays, today's throw-in is at three o'clock. The match is also being televised live by RTÉ. I arrive at the county grounds around 12.30 p.m. and the car park is beginning to fill up quite rapidly. There is good support from Down. This is certainly another step up for Wicklow. Then again, that's what we said the previous two weeks. In the dressing room I meet Kevin O'Brien who tells me that he has been up to the commentary box and that the pitch looks beautiful.

Some of the subs are coming into Noel Molloy for a rub down and for some strapping. Kevin is a bit concerned and asks Philip MacGillicuddy to marshal those coming to Noel so that the first fifteen are catered for first. Micko is reclining on the bench in his usual corner with the match programme resting on his chest. He looks totally relaxed and at peace with the universe. It evokes a distant memory of my Leaving Cert classes in Irish poetry when we learned that the ancient poets of Ireland would recline with a stone on their chests to gather inspiration.

At about twenty past one the players go out onto the pitch for their warm-up routine. Once again I am Maor Uisce 2. As the players are going through their routines I hand them the water. Most are fairly relaxed, although at the same time I can sense a slight tension.

Back in the changing room Jimmy Whittle shakes everyone's hand as they receive their jersey. Every player receives a round as applause as he accepts his jersey. Micko then speaks to the players. "Look lads, this is just another football game. Ok it's our fifth game in the championship. But lads I want you to play with fire and spirit. Put your lives on the line. Keep your eyes open. Total commitment, that's all we're asking."

As Micko is talking I sense a different atmosphere – it's almost as if there is the belief that this is a bridge too far to cross. Micko continues: "Look lads, one thing that's most important: for God's sake don't be picking the ball up off the ground. This referee is deadly. Get your foot under the ball. Forget the ref. Play the way you did the last day. Fire and guts, tackling and encouragement and shouting for each other. That's everything covered. This is a game we want to win. There are no second chances. Get our there and die for Wicklow."

When the team goes out onto the pitch there is a huge crowd present. The Down team are warming up at the goal nearest the changing rooms and Wicklow, as usual, are at the far end. The captains go to the referee for the toss and Down elect to play against the wind in the first half. I wonder if this is a bad omen – the last two Saturdays we played against the wind in the first half. The wind is quite strong today and it will be vital to be well ahead at half time. As the team gathers in the changing room for the break no one can believe it. After conceding two early points Wicklow are ahead and are controlling the game. Already Down have made a number of switches. From the sideline I have heard what their mentors have been saying to the players. Down are in trouble and they know it.

Jimmy Whittle speaks in his usual calming voice: "They have tradition. We're making it. You have done things for this county that no one else has ever done."

Leighton Glynn says: "We've two good games under our belts. Keep this pace going and they'll die."

Tony Hannon adds: "The first ten minutes are going to be crucial. Play intelligent ball. They're under pressure and they're falling over themselves."

Ciarán Hyland who has been doing a good marking job on Benny Coulter encourages the defence to make their opponents shoot from impossible angles.

Thomas Walsh, a player whom I have grown to recognise as a natural leader reminds the team of the importance of the high ball.

Half forward Jacko Dalton chips in: "Thirty-five minutes and we're into the last twelve in Ireland. Keep popping over the points."

Micko then enters the changing room with the rest of the selectors. "Paul Earls, we want you to come out and make more runs. Now lads, some of you pulled out of tackles. We're disappointed with that. For God's sake lads, go in at every shaggin' ball. James Stafford, forget about that guy. We want thirty-five minutes of total commitment. Quick and fast is the secret. Drive it in. Fight like tigers. Tony Hannon, pick up your game. Thirty-five minutes to Croke Park. You realise what's ahead. NOW GET OUT THERE AND DIE FOR WICKLOW!

Wicklow caused a sensation when they beat Down at Aughrim on Saturday to move into Round Four of the GAA All Ireland Football Qualifiers. Tony Hannon was the hero for the Garden County after his last-minute '45 gave Mick O'Dwyer's men a 1-15 to 0-17 victory. Hannon's point came about after James Stafford had failed to convert an easy chance, going for goal when he should have fisted the winning point. His shot was saved by the Down goalkeeper,

Brendan McVeigh, and was deflected for a '45, which Hannon converted to spark jubilant celebrations at 'Fortress Aughrim'. The Garden men had led 1-9 to 0-9 at the break after Leighton Glynn had struck for the only goal of the game. However, Down came back strongly in the second half and Benny Coulter levelled the game late on before Hannon intervened to save the day for Wicklow at the death. *(Report from www.gaa.ie)*

What a day. There is no greater feeling than the dressing room after winning a championship match, especially one where the victory was hard fought. Once again Micko has wielded the magic. Wicklow have now played five championship matches with another to come next week. The manager does not have to say very much to the players in the dressing room. He just tells them not to get too carried away and to stay away from alcohol. The pool in Arklow will be available in the morning and there will be training on Tuesday and Thursday.

Over an hour after the final whistle the manager is still speaking to reporters. Just when he had finished the fans wanted their time with him. The man has some charisma and stamina. At seventy-three years of age – his birthday was in June - he has time for every fan who wants an autograph or a photograph, but most of all he has most time for the children.

Tony Hannon was awarded RTÉ's man-of-the-match. I tell him that he has silenced all his critics. Today he demonstrated that he is one of the best kickers of the placed ball in the country. His injury-time forty-five against a strong breeze sailed high and far over the bar to give his side victory. Truly one of the game's gentlemen. When both Micko and Tony go out the front door of the complex the crowds are still there and the cheering is deafening. Three great victories on the trot. Back in 1975 Micko won an All Ireland after three victories: Cork, Sligo and Dublin and that was the first of eight All Irelands for that team. Also at the game this afternoon with his son was Paul McGrath, one of Ireland's greatest soccer players, who also received a rousing round of applause as he left Aughrim.

By the time Micko got to Lawless' Hotel for the post match meal many of the players had finished eating and were leaving. As the Down bus was leaving Aughrim, Kevin O'Brien was standing in the car park about thirty metres away. The Down manager, Ross Carr, against and with whom Kevin had played in the past, stopped the bus and got out. He made his way through the crowds surrounding the Wicklow selector to shake hands and congratulate him and wish the Garden County all the best in their next match. Another gentleman of the GAA.

SUNDAY 19TH JULY

The day after the sweetest victory to date: players are relaxing in the swimming pool in The Arklow Bay Hotel. It is another free Sunday, but there is the opinion that it might have been better for the lads if there were a formal training session in Aughrim – just in case any of them got slightly carried away after yesterday's victory. However when you look at what Micko has achieved who are we to question the maestro?

In the next round of the qualifiers Wicklow are drawn against Kildare while Antrim get Kerry. Last year when Wicklow won their first ever championship match in Croke Park they defeated Kieran McGeeney's Kildare. The game will be played in Portlaoise. Wicklow have happy memories of Portlaoise, as do Kildare. The stage is set for another epic battle.

TUESDAY 21ST JULY
Training in Aughrim

It's a rather cool evening in Aughrim with showers threatening. In the car park is a KLR (Kildare Local Radio) jeep sporting two lilywhite window flags. The neighbouring county's local radio station was down to do an interview with Micko. One gets the impression that Micko is still loved in Kildare. Also present is TV3 who will be doing a feature on Friday night. TV3 are also showing the game live on Saturday evening. Both Alan Byrne and Paddy Dalton are togged out and taking part in the warm up and some sprints. There follows the practice match and Alan plays a full part. Paddy stands in goal for one of the teams much to Jimmy's disappointment. Arthur and Micko sit in the away dugout and are in deep conversation. At the end of the match the maestro calls the teams together in the centre of the field.

"You're in lovely shape lads. We'll be here again on Thursday night and we'll do a little bit of kicking. Listen lads, I got a phone call late on Saturday night. Some of you were taking alcohol. I'm a bit disappointed if you were. Top athletes won't touch alcohol while they are training. Forget about the drink. You can have a few good nights when all this is over. Look lads, this run could go on for a bit yet. If anyone asks you, say it's a terrible draw. That's how we approach it. We're going to win on Saturday."

"Brian McGrath? I want you to stay in the centre at the back. Rattle 'em. Hit 'em fair and square. Now we won't say anything more because there are people listening. Isn't it amazing that we've gone three hard games and we have no injuries! There are guys on the sideline wishing for injuries! Look lads, you're all important to this team. We have thirty-four on the panel. Everyone is part of it. Everyone is willing to help out. Most of you are young. You will play for Wicklow."

Arthur then speaks: "I know Kildare fairly well. I live there and I played a bit there. There are very few Kildare players who would get on this team ahead of you." Kevin O'Brien continues: "Man for man you are better than them. Some of us live around the Kildare border. It's a great draw." Finally Martin Coleman reminds the players that if they are looking for tickets that they should place their order with him straight away. All of the stand tickets are already sold out.

THURSDAY 23RD JULY
Training in Aughrim

It is a fine evening when the session starts in Aughrim. There are quite a few spectators present and many of the cars in the car park are sporting Wicklow flags. How a little success can change a county's perception of its team. The mood is upbeat and everyone seems to be enjoying being there. No sooner has the kicking started than the rain comes. At first it seems that it will be just a short shower, but it becomes more prolonged and heavier. The view from the sideline is to leave the team kicking – sure couldn't it be raining on Saturday night? All stand tickets for Saturday are gone.

At the end of the kicking session the rain has stopped and the players gather in the centre of the pitch. Micko address them. "Now lads, you know what's ahead of us. Some years ago when I was managing Kildare we were down to thirteen men in a Leinster championship match against Laois. We went on to win that game and that was the start of a great period in Kildare. We beat Fermanagh with thirteen and I believe that that was the start of something great for Wicklow. Look lads, we have nothing to fear from Kildare. We beat them last year. Over in Kildare they are putting money on them. We are passing, running and playing for each other. Arthur and I looked at the tape of the Down game last night. Just a few small things that we need to watch. When your man has the ball we're a little bit inclined to stand off. Go in and block it. Look lads this is championship football. There is no fear in championship football. Nothing demoralises a team more than a good block. Look at Ciarán Hyland the last day. Remember no fouling. Tackle the ball. Hit the shoulder but no dragging around the neck. The man won't do any harm – it's the ball! If your man goes down on the ball in a tackle don't go down after him. Stand over him and hassle him and you'll get the free. Look lads, this is a marvellous opportunity. You're playing like champions. The last day we used Paul Earls as a third midfielder. Do you like it Paul?"

The forward-cum-third-midfielder replies that he will play wherever Micko wants him.

"James Stafford – keep running back into defence. Don't ever try a drop-kick again. (This was a reference to his effort in the dying seconds of the Down game.) The sides were level and a fisted point would have won it for Wicklow. His shot was blocked and a forty-five was awarded which Tony Hannon pointed with the last kick of the game.

"This is a game we must and want to win. We want heroes in September. I honestly believe in you. Remember, Westmeath almost beat Tyrone last year. There'll be a massive crowd in Portlaoise. It'll be like Aughrim."

Leighton Glynn says that he is looking forward to the Kildare game. "Get stuck into them from the word go. Hit with everything for the first ten minutes. Play like we did the last three days." At this stage goalkeeper Mervyn Travers arrives. Mervyn had been doing some work in his house and the clock that he was watching was an hour slow. Spotting Mervyn, Micko says: "Welcome Mervyn. Tell me how are you? Billy (reserve goalkeeper) is just wondering how you are." There is much laughter and the session comes to an end.

Tonight the post training meal is in Lawless' Hotel Aughrim as regular chef Eddie is abroad on holidays. When he booked his holidays he did not realise that Wicklow would still be involved in the championship this late in the season – oh he of little faith!

FRIDAY 24TH JULY

The ceremonial turning of the sod on Wicklow's centre of excellence project took place this evening. Work on this five million euro project is expected to start soon and will include five sand based pitches plus an all-weather Astro turf pitch. There will be a full club house, six changing rooms, gym and plunge pools. County Chairman Andy O'Brien and Wicklow GAA President

Peter Keogh performed the ceremonial turning of the sod at the sixty acre site just outside Rathdrum.

SATURDAY 25TH JULY
Fourth Round of the Qualifiers, Portlaoise
Kildare 1-16 Wicklow 2-9

The most historic day in Wicklow football has arrived – the sixth match in the football championship. The weather is bright and dry. Travelling along the N81 with Philip McGillycuddy, we notice some flowers at the side of the road marking the spot where Ciarán Shannon died in a road accident. Philip informs me that today is Ciarán's Month's Mind. When we got to Baltinglass there was a buzz about town with plenty of blue and gold bunting adorning cars, buildings and lampposts. Supporters were waiting to catch a glimpse of the team and to wish everyone well. At four o'clock the team sat down for a salad meal. Noel Molloy began his strapping routine as time would be tight by the time we got to Portlaoise.

At the end of the meal Micko stood up to address the team. "Right lads, switch off your phones once you get onto the bus and that includes you, Arthur. Now lads, I don't have to tell you about the importance of this game. Every game this year has been a big one for you. These Kildare fellas think they're All Ireland champions. It's the same team as the one we played last year. I don't have to tell you what to do. Backs keep it tight. Midfielders chat to each other. Half backs and half forwards watch for the breaks. Earley will be breaking the ball. Be competitive. Play hard but fair. Give it everything. We've got great spirit and we've had great confidence to go on in the championship. The Kildare backs aren't great so get the ball into the full forward line quick and fast. First time football. Keep tight at all times. Remember quick and fast and intelligently. There will always be players available. Let the ball go first time. For God's sake don't get sent off. We don't want any red cards. No jersey pulls. You're in peak condition, in great shape. So what if we go two, three or four points down? We've got battling qualities. Look lads I don't know what all this talk about pressure is. It's just another club match. There's no need for tension. You're as good as any team, with possibly the exception of Tyrone. Dublin and Kildare are talking of the All Ireland final. We'll bate the shite outta them. Let's go."

There is a garda car waiting to escort us. As we turn towards Castledermot there is a large blue and yellow sign that says: "Best of luck to Micko and the Wicklow football team from Fergus Kenny." Fergus had repaired a puncture for Micko during the week. Supporters are out along the route and cheer the bus as it passes. Once we cross the border into Kildare there is a mixture of colours. Apparently Kevin O'Brien's brother bought up plenty of blue and yellow paint and made good use of it. Earlier in the week Jimmy Whittle and his brother "reclaimed" the bridge near the kit man's house with Wicklow flags and bunting, the last house this side of the border between the two counties. Later Jimmy's brother decided to climb a tree to hang some more flags. Unfortunately he fell out of the tree and ended up in hospital with two broken arms. When we reached the roundabout at the Carlow bypass the garda car returned to Baltinglass. The comment from one team member was: "They can't be out of Balto for too long on the crime rate rises." Just outside of Stradbally two garda motor cyclists meet us. They will escort us into Portlaoise.

When we arrive at O'Moore Park the Wexford-Clare relegation hurling match is well into the second half. Clare will win and the once mighty hurling power of Wexford will be fighting for survival. The warm-up routines take place on the pitches behind the stand. Once again I am Maor Uisce 2 so I am giving out the water-bottles to the players. On the pitch next to us Kildare are warming up.

The jerseys are given out to the usual rounds of applause. Micko calls the team to stand around the table in the centre of the room. He tells us that Arthur would like to say a few words. The

Maor Fóirne calls for a minute's silence in memory of Fr. Tom. Arthur asks the players to thank him and to ask the late priest to guide them from above today. Following the silence Micko says that we have covered everything. "This is a game that will take us to Croke Park. We know them. Last year we played them off the pitch. NOW GET OUT THERE AND DIE FOR WICKLOW!"

At half time Jimmy Whittle speaks in his concentrated quiet way. "Take everything good out of the first half. They got feck all with that wind: four points. If this was a club game you'd be clapping yourselves on the back coming in here just four points down at half time. Leighton takes up the encouraging theme: "We didn't play as we could. Fact: we're four points down against a strong wind. They're rattled. The goal shook them. Send the ball in and Deano and Seánie will fucking destroy them. Our work rate wasn't good. Up the work rate and we'll get on top."

Jacko Dalton adds: "I want to play in an All Ireland quarter final. Work like hell. Get two points and they'll drop."

Half back Padge McWalter tells us: "They don't like it when we run at them." Jimmy Whittle gives the scoring facts from the championship so far: 2-12 against Longford, 1-10 against Westmeath, 0-17 against Fermanagh, 1-12 against Cavan, 1-15 against Down. "They're the statistics. And we're going to get more tonight."

As soon as the manager comes into the changing room everyone stands up. "Now lads, we're not going to make any switches. Half backs, quick and fast. Their full back line is not good. Defenders get the ball into the forwards. Quick and fast ball. Their full back is not good. Look lads, we have thirty-five minutes. We've a good wind behind us this half but the wind won't win it for us. The ball has been knocked out of our hands a few times because we're holding it out there. Into the chest. Don't spill anything. NOW GET OUT THERE AND DIE FOR WICKLOW!"

The final whistle has sounded and now there is silence and tears in the changing room. When Micko comes in he asks for the door to be closed and he addresses his troops: "Look lads, you have nothing to be ashamed of. Don't be downhearted. Stay with it. You play a great brand of football. A little bit of luck and we'd have beaten them. You have made a wonderful contribution to Wicklow. You are a credit to your county. Keep with it and you'll succeed." To me that sounded like a farewell speech. Hopefully it was not because what has been achieved in Wicklow over the last three years is unbelievable. Six matches in the championship and coming within a few minutes of an All Ireland quarter final this year. This has been Wicklow's most successful season ever under the guidance of the country's most successful manager.

County chairman Andy O'Brien addressed the gathering, "Tonight is a night to take a rest. I want to thank you for your effort and commitment. You have made an untold impression on the children of Wicklow. Young people are looking up to you. The county wants you to keep going. Take a break tonight. All those nights in the muck in places like Annacurra and Knockananna during the winter paid off. Well done."

Team captain Leighton then speaks: "I'd like to thank Mick O'Dwyer and the back room staff. You made a difference to Wicklow. We're as sick as dogs. With a little bit of luck we would have won. Look at what has been achieved over the last three years. Look what will be achieved over the next five years. I've three or four years of football left in me. We're proud men and let's keep it going for the sake of Wicklow."

Micko is still available to meet and greet the fans and to give interviews. He is still signing jerseys, hats and programmes. Even in defeat he is a pure gentleman and is no doubt considering his future. Fans are still waiting to cheer on the team as they make their way to the bus. www.gaa.ie reports:

Mick O'Dwyer's overriding emotion was one of pride after Wicklow's gutsy GAA All Ireland Round Four defeat to Kildare on Saturday night. After a remarkable second half fight back, the pin was finally pricked in the Garden County's Championship dreams only after Alan Smith's late goal for the Lilywhites.

Kildare manager Kieran McGeeney then came into the Wicklow changing room. The first thing he did was to apologise to Wicklow for his behaviour the previous year. After Wicklow defeated his Kildare team in Croke Park there was the opinion that he had snubbed Wicklow. "I didn't snub Wicklow. I was new to management. As a player I know what it's like to lose. Thank you for a great game and you are a credit to your county. Your four games on the trot made the difference. You are a fantastic team with fantastic pace out of defence. Again I want to apologise for last year."

Sitting on the bus outside the ground I had the opportunity to reflect on this seven month journey. In the quiet of the bus I could see the pain and disappointment of the players, management and supporters. Brian McGrath, Dean Odlum, Seánie Furlong and Mervyn Travers were standing outside at the front of the bus. Mervyn was inconsolable. When a team loses a close game after conceding a very late goal there is nothing that anyone can say to the goalkeeper. Regardless of the circumstances a goalkeeper will always blame himself for conceding a decisive late goal. No words will console him despite the fact that he has made numerous vital saves for his team throughout the season.

In O'Loughlin's Hotel owner Declan O'Loughlin was none too pleased with some of the decisions that were made against Wicklow. James Stafford in particular came in for some rough treatment and Thomas Walsh was blown up on a number of occasions for allegedly over carrying the ball. Paul Earls was the subject of a high and heavy tackle during the second half and play was waved on. It seems that when you are the underdog marginal decisions are not the only ones that will go against you. Arthur addressed the panel just before the end of the meal. "This has been an incredible three year journey. I came into it through a trick a man played. I was to be in the stand and far away. It has been the greatest pleasure of my life to have been involved with you lads. It has been an honour to work at first hand with the greatest legend in Gaelic football. I want to thank him and I want to thank the back room team. You know what it's like - a circus and a training camp and we mixed it and sometimes we got it right. I saw Mick O'Dwyer in his prime at left half back and then as a forward and the rest is history. You should hear what people all over Ireland are saying. The Wicklow story has been the most romantic story in the history of the GAA. Forevermore you did yourselves proud. Lots of people say that it was unusual that we used the same fifteen and no subs. I was a sub too. When you go back to your clubs play like you never played before. This team is worth getting on. I was a sub and I know what it is like. All arguments can be solved on the field of play. Lads, it has been a pleasure working with you and if there is ever anything I can ever do for you, just let me know." Was that another farewell speech?

The bus journey back to Baltinglass was a mixture of emotions. Some were quiet reminiscing perhaps on what might have been and of course on what had been achieved. Some were unable to speak and some were beginning to put it behind them. There was disappointment but there was also an upbeat feeling. When we got to Baltinglass there were people waiting to cheer on the team. As we took our bags out of the bus players said good bye to each other and drifted away. We shook hands with each other and wished each other well. I saw Micko drive off and wondered if that was it. Would he come back to Wicklow for one more year and bring us on yet further still? If anyone can do it the greatest living legend in Gaelic football can.

CHAPTER NINE

What Happened Next?

AFTER the exploits of July 2009, there were some more highlights from Wicklow's most memorable year. In addition to Tony Hannon winning the Vodafone Player Man of the Match award for his performance against Down, he also received the Irish Independent Sports Star of the Week. Both Ciarán Hyland and Leighton Glynn received All Star nominations, but unfortunately neither was selected.

Micko and Arthur announced that they would stay with Wicklow for one more season and see if the team could go further in 2010. As 2009 came to an end hopes and expectations for 2010 were high. To add further to the expectations when the draw for the 2010 championship was made Wicklow were put in the "easier" side of the draw. The first match would be against Carlow with the winners playing Westmeath. A Leinster Final was a distinct possibility. Roll on 2010.

The season began with an O'Byrne Cup match in Baltinglass against Louth. Jimmy Whittle was now a selector replacing Philip McGillicuddy who stepped down at the end of 2009. Louth won on a scoreline of 2-18 to 0-11. However this was a largely experimental side with a number of new faces. The next game was in the O'Byrne Shield away to Carlow. Wicklow lost 2-13 to 1-10. Nobody was going to read too much into this game – both sides would have to play each other twice more before the year was over, once in the league and in the all-important opening match of the Leinster Championship. At the time there was uncertainty about

Thomas Walsh. Rumours were circulating that he had moved back to Carlow and would be transferring back to his home county.

The first game of the National League was away to Clare. Wicklow led comfortably by the mid point of the second half but then conceded a goal. This gave Clare new life and they won by a point in injury time. A disappointing start to the league and already promotion was going to be difficult. Things picked up but we lost a match at home to Leitrim on a score of 1-13 to 0-9. Playing for Leitrim in the number 10 jersey that day was Philip McGuinness. Two months later Philip died in following a serious head injury sustained in a club game while playing for Mohill. Ar dheis de go raibh a anam.

The third game of the league saw Wicklow travel to Ruislip to play London. Seánie Furlong scored 3-2 of Wicklow's 4-13. The Garden County conceded just 1-5. Round four saw the second meeting of Wicklow and Carlow. This time the venue was Aughrim where Wicklow won 0-14 to 0-7. Round five saw Wicklow travel to Pearse Park in Longford. This was always going to be a tricky assignment. Victory here would put Wicklow very much in contention for promotion. Wicklow played some superb football in the second half and won by a point 2-9 to 1-11.

It was now back to Aughrim to face promotion-chasing Limerick. A draw was to be the final result, Wicklow scoring 14 points to Limerick's 1-11. The next game was away to Waterford. Victory here would almost certainly guarantee promotion. The final round of the league would see Wicklow at home to Kilkenny, a match Wicklow won comfortably 2-25 to 0-7. Wicklow seemed to be in control after 30 minutes but then Waterford's ace marksman Liam Ó Lionáin netted twice before half time. Wicklow were struggling from then on and eventually lost 2-17 to 1-11. Promotion from division four was lost here. Waterford and Limerick were promoted to division three. With the league programme completed it was now time to concentrate on the big one – Carlow in Portlaoise in the Leinster Championship.

Much media coverage concentrated on the midfield of Carlow – Brendan Murphy and the ex-Wicklow footballer Thomas Walsh. Carlow were seen to be the favourites, but if there is one thing that Micko can do it is prepare a team for the championship. This he did and Wicklow won on a scoreline of 3-13 to 0-12. Both Carlow midfielders were sent off. But this victory came at a huge cost to Wicklow. Padge McWalter was stretched off in the second half with a very serious knee injury. In fact this injury not only finished the half back's season but kept him out of action for the 2011 season as well.

The next round of the Leinster Championship saw a repeat of the previous year's fixture: Westmeath in Tullamore. Wicklow were fancied to do well in this game. In fact such was the interest in this game that the gardaí had the throw-in delayed for fifteen minutes to allow the supporters get into the ground. When the game finally did get underway Wicklow were very lethargic: with ten minutes to go Westmeath were six points ahead. Wicklow had suffered yet another serious blow when goalkeeper Mervyn Travers was stretchered off with a serious knee injury. At the corresponding fixture twelve months previously Wicklow suffered three serious injuries in as many minutes. Was this the curse of Tullamore revisiting Micko's men? But Wicklow suddenly woke up and levelled the match. However there was to be no joy for the Garden County. In the third minute of injury time Westmeath clinched what was to be the winning point. Wicklow lost 0-15 to 1-11. Rather than advancing in the Leinster Championship Wicklow would be playing in the qualifiers.

Round One of the Qualifiers saw Wicklow travel to Brefini Park to take on Cavan. At half time Wicklow were leading 2-6 to 0-5 and were a man to the good. Shortly after the restart Cavan were reduced to thirteen men and it looked as if the Garden County would be progressing to round two of the qualifiers. Sadly this was not to be: Cavan powered back into the game and Seánie Johnson who came on as a sub in the second half went on a scoring spree raising six white flags. Wicklow only managed two points in the entire second half and exited the championship 0-15 to 2-8.

Micko never said definitively that he had terminated his links with Wicklow. During the remainder of the summer there was much speculation about whether he would return to Wicklow or not for one more season. His name was linked with some counties where there were managerial vacancies, especially Mayo. With Arthur being from Mayo it seemed that the Waterville Maestro's future might lie west of the Shannon. It was early September before we knew what his intentions were. Micko was going to stay for one more year and give promotion from division four a good effort. Arthur was stepping down and would be replaced as selector by Martin Coleman. When questioned about why he had delayed saying that he would be staying with Wicklow, Micko cheekily said that he never said that he was finished with Wicklow.

When the draw for the Leinster Championship was made Wicklow were placed in the difficult side of the draw. First up would be a meeting with Kildare with the winners taking on Meath. The winners of this would then meet the winners of Dublin and Laois or Longford in a Leinster semi-final. There was no dream draw for Wicklow in 2011.

The 2011 season began with a trip to O'Moore Park to take on Laois in the O'Byrne Cup. With an experimental side Wicklow played some lovely football and won the tie 1-10 to 1-9. Next up was an away match to Louth which was also televised live. This was a competitive tie which the home side won 2-13 to 1-12. Replacement goalkeeper John Flynn gave an excellent display in goal and saved a first half penalty. The following week there was a challenge match against UCC in Rathinesky GAA Grounds outside Stradbally in Laois. The university team won this match. In fact UCC, under the guidance of Cork All Ireland winner and manager Billy Morgan went on to win the 2011 Sigerson Cup.

The league began in February with an away match to Carlow. At full time the scoreline read Carlow 2-10 Wicklow 1-13. This was the first time that I had been to a game in Dr. Cullen Park that Wicklow did not lose. The next match was also an away tie, this time to Leitrim, a difficult assignment. Wicklow won the game 1-15 to 1-10. The first home game was against London which Wicklow won comfortably 2-22 to 1-4. Promotion from the basement division was a distinct possibility. Round four saw Wicklow travel to Fermanagh for a difficult assignment. A draw was the result with Fermanagh scoring 0-13 to Wicklow's 2-7. The second week of March saw Wicklow at home to Longford – a tricky assignment. Another valuable league point was lost when the the Longford team came from a five point deficit in the second half to register 1-12 to the home side's 2-9. A week later Wicklow were away to Kilkenny where the Garden county registered just a second victory in the league 4-16 to 1-5. This was a very costly victory though. Stephen "Chester" Kelly received a straight red which meant he would not be able to play for the remainder of the league. Also Padge McWalterplayed in this match but would not play again for the remainder of the season. His knee had still not recovered. A Wicklow team without Padge is a severely weakened team. With two home matches still left to play promotion was still within our own grasp.

The first was against Connacht champions Roscommon who had no intention of staying in divisin four for more than one season. Well into the second half Wicklow were leading by five points but were at the losing end of a 3-14 to 2-16 scoreline. In fact this is the only match that Wicklow lost in the entire league campaign in 2011 – a one point loss to the 2010 Connacht champions. Promotion was still a possibility as Wicklow faced Clare in the final round of the league. If we could win and if Carlow could beat Longford away Roscommon and Wicklow would be promoted. Alas Wicklow once again drew in a high scoring game 1-17 to Clare's 0-20. Had Wicklow won promotion would still have eluded us as Carlow were beaten by nine points. In the division four final played in Croke Park Longford defeated Roscommon.

With the league out of the way it was full steam ahead for the opening match of the 2011 Leinster campaign against Kildare. This game was played in Portlaoise, the venue where Wicklow's 2009 qualifier run came to an end in round four against the same opposition. It was also shown live on television. After a promising first half Wicklow fell away and eventually lost on a scoreline of 0-12 to 0-5. Kildare had eighteen wides and Wicklow's only point of the second half was in injury time. In Micko's five seasons in charge this was the first time his team were beaten in the first game of the championship. There was much criticism of the team and its performance following this defeat. Wicklow would now have to wait for five weeks before the first round of the qualifiers. To rub salt into the wounds, Wicklow's latest recruit, Austin O'Malley from Mayo, was shown a straight red card and was unavailable for the next game.

When the draw for the first round of qualifiers was made Wicklow were given a home match against Sligo. Sligo had beaten Wicklow by a point in the league in 2009 and were promoted to division three. They then went on to win the Connacht championship. In 2010 they gained promotion to division two but were subsequently beaten by Roscommon in the Connacht Final. Although they were relegated to division three at the end of the 2011 league many felt that Sligo would make progress through the qualifiers. In fact all six sports writers in the match programme for the Wicklow-Sligo tie tipped Sligo to win. Following the Garden County's performance against Kildare five weeks previously very few people gave Wicklow any hope of winning. But Micko has been around for a long, long time and he got his team just right for the match. Wicklow won by five points and played some excellent football. The final score was 1-18 to 0-16. Was there going to be a repeat of 2009? Popular opinion before this match was that this would be Micko's final game in charge of Wicklow.

In round two of the qualifiers Wicklow were drawn away to Armagh. Armagh and Tyrone have dominated the Ulster

Championship for over ten years and between have won four All Irelands in the same period. This time the popular opinion was that Micko's reign would come to an end following the game in the Morgan Athletic Grounds. Wicklow tried to have the game brought forward from 7.00 p.m. to 5.00 p.m. but this request was not upheld. On a warm balmy night in Armagh, Wicklow took the game to Armagh and were leading at half-time. Armagh were shell shocked but in the second half came out with all guns blazing. They scored eight points without reply and with minutes left to play led by two points. Seánie Furlong found the net with time almost up and incredibly Wicklow were ahead by a point. Unfortunately in injury time Aaron Kernan snatched an equalising point to force extra time. In the first period of extra time Armagh dominated and seemed set for a two point victory. But in an almost carbon copy of the final moments of normal time Furlong once again found the net. Wicklow were ahead by a point. However similarities with normal time continued and once again Aaron Kernan managed an equalizing point. The full time whistle sounded. Micko's men had once again done the incredible and forced a replay. James Stafford gave an outstanding performance in midfield and was lauded by one and all. Wicklow supporters went home delighted with the prospect of another crack at Armagh in Aughrim. When the Wicklow bus returned to the Green Isle Hotel after midnight everyone was looking forward to a good night's sleep.

Micko got into his car and drove to Waterville where he teed off in the Captain's Prize at 7.20 a.m. From where does he get his energy?

Over 7,000 people packed the county grounds in Aughrim to cheer on Micko's men. However in Gaelic games the underdog seldom comes out top in a replay. In the last training session before the game Staff fell awkwardly on his ankle. In fact he was only passed fit to play shortly before the throw-in. Even though he was fit to play and gave another tremendous performance, he was clearly not firing on all cylinders. To further add to Wicklow's woes,

Jacko Dalton who gave a sterling performance in Armagh pulled his troublesome hamstring in the warm-up. However, the first fifteen minutes a shock seemed possible. After trailing by two points early on Wicklow scored four points without reply. But then in the nineteenth minute Armagh got a goal from which Wicklow never really recovered. In the second half Wicklow continued to fight but when Armagh scored a second goal the result seemed inevitable. After five glorious seasons Micko's men surrendered their unbeaten championship run in Aughrim under the maestro to Armagh on a scoreline of 2-9 to 0-10.

Gerry Grehan wrote in The Wicklow Times:

It's five past 10 on Saturday the 16th July. Micko is walking out of the Aughrim dressing room for the last time as Wicklow Manager. It was all a little bit sad. Three hours earlier there were 7,000 people in the grounds, now we are down to the last dozen. Dave Barrett takes a final photo of Micko, Michael Sargent, and myself. Micko walks with Martin Coleman to his car and they drive away. And just like that, the Micko journey is over.

CHAPTER TEN

Dramatis Personae

DURING my access to the Wicklow team in 2009, I interviewed the management and several other people connected with the team.

JIMMY WHITTLE

Jimmy is always first to training and last to leave. As I got to know him during my time with the Wicklow team I began to help him with gathering up equipment, bibs and footballs after training. By the time we got to Aughrim in April, I usually collected the footballs and brought them to the store. Jimmy always thanked me and never took anything for granted.

He is one of those gentlemen who goes about his duties in a quiet and unassuming way, yet behind this exterior is a wit that can take and give as much as the loudest comedians in the panel. He also has a love of local history and will often inform and educate those who are willing to listen to him, and, as always, in a most unassuming way.

About a month after Wicklow's exit from the championship, I interviewed him. Jimmy played at all age levels for the Dunlavin club and also played national hurling and football league for the county. While living and working in Dublin in the mid-1970s Jimmy played with the Ballyboden St. Enda's Club in south county Dublin. Jimmy role with Wicklow was officially termed "The Kit Manager" for the first team and selector for the second (junior) team. Like the U-21s, he sees the junior structure as a type of conveyor belt that leads to senior football.

During his tenure players like Derek Daly, Rory Nolan, Darren Hayden and Stephen "Chester" Kelly progressed through the ranks to make an impact on the senior team. He sees the junior team as giving quality match practice to fringe players. This year was by far the most successful yet for Wicklow in the senior ranks, thanks in no small way to the commitment of the junior team. Jimmy had been part of the back room team during Hugh Kenny's final year. When Micko came on board he was asked to stay. He did not need much persuasion. He felt that striving for success was motivation enough to stay under the new manager. He had expectations and dreams of achieving goals and targets that Wicklow never met before. He felt that if Wicklow could make the breakthrough success could influence and change people.

In the qualifiers Wicklow beat three Ulster teams – beating three Ulster teams would be enough to win the Ulster title. The Westmeath game was a blip on the radar screen – it was one of those days when anything that could have gone wrong did go wrong. Yet it was a blessing in disguise – it opened the proverbial backdoor to the qualifiers. Longford in the first round of the Leinster championship was a banana skin: Wicklow snatched victory from the jaws of defeat – how many times has it been the other way for Wicklow?

Micko's presence was felt from day one. Once he had been appointed manager expectations rose. Attendances at matches rose. Jimmy feels that the key ingredient in Micko's arsenal is respect. He gets players to respect each other. He shows respect to everyone. The best person in any organisation should be the chief executive. That is Micko.

Jimmy's most memorable moment during the three years was the victory over Kildare. The proverbial monkey had been taken off the Wicklow back. For the first time, everything came together for a Wicklow team in Croke Park. Tony Hannon's point against Down was another highlight, as was winning the Tommy Murphy Cup in 2007. Indeed Jimmy feels that Hannon's winning point was almost a gift to Micko in appreciation for everything that he had done for the team over the last three years. Micko is the best GAA man in the country and his coming to Wicklow could be compared to Sir Alex Ferguson taking over the reigns at Burton Albion. And people did give their all under Micko. This was emphasised beyond all doubt following the final whistle in the Down match when tears were shed by old and young alike, players, backroom team and supporters. The difference was, this time, these were tears of joy.

The defeat to Laois in 2008 was Jimmy's biggest disappointment. Disappointments in the past usually meant that Wicklow took giant steps backwards. Under Micko this trend was reversed. There was disappointment but the team bounced back and qualified for the Tommy Murphy Cup final. Against Fermanagh this year the team dug into their reserves to win with thirteen men. The next morning all but two players were in Aughrim for training – one absentee was working and the other was carrying an injury.

Jimmy never considered quitting at any time: his philosophy was simply, if Micko can make those sacrifices, so can I. Jimmy related an story about the demands of travelling. One Saturday evening in winter training finished in Aughrim at 4.30 p.m. Training was to be in Kilmacanogue at 11.00 a.m. the next morning. Jimmy drove home to Dunlavin and the next morning drove to training – a journey of over an hour. He arrived at 10.10 a.m. in plenty of time, only to find Micko already there. Since the previous evening Micko had driven to Galway, presented medals at a function and was back in Kilmac the next morning for training before anyone else had arrived. Micko never missed a training session, even when the weather was bad. He was always there ahead of everyone else. As Jimmy says, with enthusiasm like that who'd need insulin?

The profile of the county was raised beyond all expectations. Supporters came in their droves to observe training. Media personnel came to Aughrim on Tuesday and Thursday nights.

There was a huge increase in the sale of county jerseys. Jimmy feels that he was lucky to have been chosen to work for the county. With regard to business life, he feels that his involvement with the team did help. He regards the dressing room as being similar to the board room. His employers did not hinder him, but rather wished him well. He was always able to return to work.

And what of the criticisms of Micko's "old fashioned" training methods? Jimmy says that to start a long journey in the car you need a full tank. The team needs seven months for 70 minutes. Eight All Irelands and provincial titles with three counties? He has ample proof that his methods work. Early season training is to get the body fit. The sharpness follows when the evenings get longer. This year Wicklow never fell away in the last fifteen minutes of any match. The slog of winter training in all weathers brings its own mental strength too. None of the backroom team could refuse a request from Micko. He delegated well and showed respect for all. Micko was the boss, but he allowed the selectors to scout for him. All opinions were considered.

But Micko didn't use any subs in the qualifiers and that's why we lost to Kildare? Fringe players were given opportunities but the best fifteen had to be selected for championship. Players are ambitious but they also have to be patient. The fifteen on the bench are every bit as important as the fifteen on the pitch. Some players have to bide their time for years before getting their reward.

Fr. Tom had a profound influence on Jimmy. The friar came with Arthur and became a friend and chaplain to the team. Not only that, he was a friend and confidant to many people in the wider GAA community. He seemed to be quiet and dignified, but Jimmy believes that the late priest always knew more than he said. He would say Mass in The Glenview Hotel before big games. He was in the hearts and minds of the team this year. He was always mentioned in the dressing room. Jimmy hopes that this year we made Fr. Tom happy. Wicklow was this priest's last project. When

Tony Hannon stepped up to take that famous forty-five against Down, Jimmy grabbed Arthur's hand and whispered "Fr. Tom will guide this over." The rest, as the cliché goes, is history.

"The strength of Wicklow is endurance," he said. "Wicklow was the last county to be colonised. Anne Devlin from Corballis, near Rathdrum, endured years in prison because of her loyalty to Robert Emmet. Michael Dwyer spent five years causing havoc in the Wicklow Mountains and only surrendered when he realised that to continue would only bring worse hardship on his county. That's what Wicklow have – an awareness of place."

TEAM ADMINISTRATOR: MARTIN COLEMAN

Martin Coleman comes from south Carlow near the Kilkenny border. Work brought him to Baltinglass where he began to play hurling and football with Kiltegan. He never played at county level. Rather, his playing was confined to the ranks of the juniors and intermediates. He experienced success in local championships and district leagues. Martin began to fill various roles in the Baltinglass Club. He became PRO and later Assistant Secretary. He became Secretary in 1987, a role he filled for eighteen years. He was also West Juvenile Chairman for five years and held various positions within the county over the years.

Martin had been team administrator under Hugh Kenny's management. Local TD, and Baltinglass Clubman, Billy Timmons had a word in Martin's ear and asked him to consider staying on under Micko. Billy said he'd give Martin two weeks to think about the offer, but during those two weeks Martin would receive two phone calls a day from his local public representative. He finally agreed that working with Micko was too good an opportunity to reject. He accepted and never looked back. As Martin says, "A week after Micko took over the circus began." The first panel of over a hundred and twenty players was considered in Billy Timmons' Dáil office by Kevin, Philip and Martin. The following Saturday the first training session was held.

Martin tells me that Micko was alarmed at the low level of skill of the players. Micko had come to increase the profile of the county and to lift the fortunes of Wicklow GAA. There was a tremendous media frenzy in the Westbury Hotel when Micko was unveiled as the latest Wicklow manager. The most successful manager in the history of the GAA was taking over the reins of the least successful county.

From Micko's first training session, the emphasis was always on the championship. After three years how does Martin feel that these aims were met?

Certainly the county's profile has never been higher and in 2009 the team progressed to the last twelve of the All Ireland. He remarks that in one of the Vodafone TV ads there is a scene of a father and son wearing Wicklow jerseys skipping into Croke Park. In another ad you can see a scoreboard for a Wicklow v Kerry match. Without Micko this level of media interest would not have happened. Micko was adamant that during his tenure Wicklow would always be to the fore.

Was Micko only in it for the money? Martin states that the manager never looked for anything. For example, if a football went missing at training he would ask Jimmy Whittle had it been found. Micko hates waste, and he hates to see a county board's cash being wasted. He visited numerous clubs and development squads throughout the county and never asked for a penny. Micko deserves plenty of monetary reward but he never looks for it.

According to Martin, Micko should be a paid ambassador for the GAA. On the occasion of his visit to Baltinglass Hospital, an elderly Valleymount resident, Tommy Tipper, who was a day patient at the time, refused to go home until he met Micko. The photographs from that day are still hanging in the hospital. Micko has the ability to lift everyone's spirits. His enthusiasm for life is infectious. Martin tells me that one evening in Aughrim he noticed a man in his forties whom he knew. This man was wearing a Wicklow jersey – for the first time in his life.

Martin will stay if Micko stays. With regard to not using any subs, Martin says that the dilemma was "Who would you take off?" He feels that the players on the bench need another season of training to bring them up to the required level. Martin says that Micko reminds him of a good farmer with stock. An amazing ability of Micko is to ref and see a player at the same time. It is an amazing ability to be able to read players and a game from the centre of the pitch.

Micko's philosophy is simple: get the body in shape and kick football. Win the ball and play it. It is a system that worked in Kerry, Kildare, Laois and more recently with Wicklow. No other manager could get players to run lap after lap, but Micko could. At all stages during the 2009 championship, Wicklow were able to keep on going right up until the final whistle.

From day one of this year he emphasised the importance of 24th May 2009 in Portlaoise. He would talk to the critics that night. The league is simply another set of training sessions for Micko. Back in January Micko remarked that Darren Hayden, a young player who shone in the qualifiers, was not playing in his best position. At the time Micko felt that this player should be playing wing back. How accurate the manager was. Micko did not want the team to peak for the league – there were bigger challenges ahead in the summer.

When one looks at Micko's three years in charge, there can be very little criticism of the championship performances: three matches against Louth in 2007, victory over Kildare in 2008 followed by the disappointment of the Laois game, and then that glorious run to the last twelve in 2009. The defeat to Westmeath, while painful at the time, was the making of the team. Following that defeat, attendance at training was almost always one hundred per cent. Martin feels that the team would not have gotten the run had they been victorious in Tullamore.

There were never extra demands placed on the Team Administrator. He felt that he had a duty, but it was a duty that was willingly and lovingly carried out. Whatever you did you did, and nothing was ever a problem for Micko.

Martin thinks about the most memorable moments from the last three years – its takes a little time because there were so many. He smiles when he thinks of the little boy who asked Micko to sign his cap for him after one of the qualifiers in Aughrim. Micko obliged and the young lad looked up at the manager and says, "You're a great man Micko!" The night in The Wagon Wheel in Knockananna when Micko played the button accordion was also memorable, as was the vocal support in Portlaoise for the Kildare match, even though the Garden County's supporters were outnumbered. Following that defeat there was no negativity – the only question was "Will he stay?" The times when Micko would break into song were also memorable, The Leaving of Dingle being a favourite. No, there were no regrets for Martin. How could there be with so many great results? Fr. Tom loved his involvement with the team. Before the Laois game in 2008 he was in a nursing home in Dublin, but managed to drive to Baltinglass to wish the team well before they left for the game.

Other notable individuals who were met along the way was the then US Ambassador to Ireland, Tom Foley, who came into the dressing room following the Tommy Murphy Cup victory. Arthur, a man with many contacts was known to take phone calls from well known individuals after a game – Charlie McCreevy and Martin McAleese, to name but two.

The Tommy Murphy Cup helped to get the county to where it is now. The 2007 Tommy Murphy Cup campaign was very important, but by 2008 it had lost its appeal. The county had been there and had done that. It was time to move on.

Martin never considered quitting at any stage. Lack of self-confidence and self-belief were rife in Wicklow before Micko's arrival. Micko is a practical psychologist. Counties pay large fees for professional psychologists to assist with team preparation. What Micko does is give self-confidence and self-belief to a player.

He feels that the county needs to market Micko better than it has done to date. Arthur has a most important role to play here. Martin hopes and prays that both Arthur and Micko see that their work is not yet finished and that we have more glorious years ahead.

WICKLOW GAA PRESIDENT: PETER KEOGH

What can one say about Peter Keogh? Peter is the elder statesman of Wicklow GAA and columnist and match reporter with The Wicklow People "for more years than I care to remember". Peter has been President of Wicklow GAA since the late 1980s. Peter told me: "It's a job they give you to get rid of you." It's an ambassadorial role with restrictions. He is the successor in this role to Billy Lawless and Hugh Byrne. One of the conditions of presidency is that the incumbent has no vote. Peter was born in Talbotstown where he lived for twenty years. When he married he moved to Kiltegan where he has resided ever since. Peter became a columnist with the Wicklow People by accident. Dinny Kelly from Dunlavin had been secretary of the west county board for twenty-one years. When Peter became the secretary Dinny wrote up the notes for the local paper. Following Dinny's death in the early 1980s, Hillary Murphy of the Wicklow People asked Peter to do the notes for a couple of weeks "until they got themselves sorted out." Peter believes that they still haven't sorted themselves out!

I met Peter on a Saturday in late August, in his kitchen, taking him away from writing his Keogh's Corner article for The Wicklow People. Later that day he would be reporting on various club games for the local paper. When I asked Peter about the coming of the Messiah he said that there had been rumours circulating in late 2006 that Micko would be coming to Wicklow, but that he, Peter Keogh, did not believe them. He says that did not know a lot about Mick O'Dwyer, apart from what was known of him as being the most highly decorated manager in gaelic games. On the day that Micko was unveiled as the new Wicklow manager there was a press conference in The Westbury Hotel in Dublin. Micko was sitting between County Chairman Mick Hagan and County Administrator Michael Murphy.

Wicklow had had good managers and trainers in the past. In the early years of this decade Wicklow had had a high profile "outsider" as manager, namely Dublin All Ireland winning captain, John O'Leary, but this did not work out. However, when the Waterville maestro was unveiled as the new Wicklow manager the buzz and media attention reached an all-time high. True, Wicklow had had media attention in the past, but usually it was for the wrong reasons.

Since Micko's first training session, the improvements were instantly noticeable. What impressed Peter so much was that everything that was achieved was done so in good humour. Never did there appear to be any pressure on anyone. John O'Leary was calm and good-humoured, but Micko was exceptional. Peter knew of Micko's talent as a player and as a manager, but coming to Wicklow gave the President the opportunity to get to know the Kerryman as a person. "He was an absolute gem to work with. He never refused to meet with anyone, either journalist or child, even when he was busy. He never refused a club or individual within in reach. Schools, hospitals, the old and the young: he lifted everyone's spirits in Wicklow."

Micko never took a cent from any club, school or hospital. Money never mattered to Micko. Peter says that whenever he hears of a managerial vacancy that he gets a cold chill running down his spine. Micko's presence ensured a good sponsorship for the county team. But Micko is not a solo act: there is Arthur French who is Micko's greatest friend. Peter reminds me of how Wicklow TD Billy Timmons met Arthur at a funeral and how the chat turned to football. Arthur met Billy at the funeral of the TD's uncle. Billy's uncle had lived close to Arthur in Leixlip. Arthur had been with Micko in Laois, but only stayed three weeks. Arthur did not like Laois, but he loved Wicklow. Arthur has done a huge amount for Wicklow behind the scenes. For example, following the Tommy

Murphy Cup victory the Wicklow team travelled to New York. Arthur was responsible for securing much sponsorship for this visit stateside. Arthur also had many contacts in New York. In Peter's opinion, Arthur was the right man at the right time for Wicklow football.

Peter is not critical of Micko's so-called old-fashioned methods of training. He refers to Kilkenny where Brian Cody's methods are similar to those of the Kerryman. Cody also referees training matches as does Micko. Neither the Kilkennyman nor the Wicklow managers are too inclined to blow for fouls during training matches.

Micko has his methods. Training matches consist of backs and forwards with little time for challenge matches - a similar philosophy to that of Kerry and Kilkenny. Peter regards criticism as part and parcel of team management. When there is success selections are justified. At the end of the championship there can only be one champion – there will always be thirty-one disappointed counties. After a defeat management will be criticised by the "should have" brigade. Criticism is par for the course and Peter says that he has had to endure it all his life – when great teams come to the end of their success the management will be blamed.

My final question to Peter is: "Why has Wicklow not been successful?"He says that there is no short answer. On paper Wicklow should be up there with the big names. The GAA started in the Garden County in the 1880s, one of the first counties to be established. Peter feels that before the advent of modern methods transport travel in the county was difficult because of the mountainous terrain. The GAA was run from Wicklow Town and the pony and trap was the preferred method of transport for those who could afford it. Also the country was only recovering from the drastic effects of the famine. Even horses need to take rests on the journey from east to west and vice versa. In the early days of the GAA there were twenty-one players on a team - the logistics of transport were indeed a headache. Matches were often played in The Bottoms in Rathdrum, but it was difficult to get a team to the venue – players had to walk across the mountains. Wicklow GAA began with a bang in 1887 long before many other counties got started. However, Peter feels that the initial enthusiasm eventually waned when the reality of travelling to matches set in. For the first twenty-five years of the GAA in Wicklow there was no involvement from the west of the county. The first west Wicklow representative on the county board was Matt Byrne who had a car. In 1910 the west got its own board. In 1911 Valleymount won the junior championship, and Baltinglass won it a year later. In 1915 Blessington won their first senior championship. The success of the west was copied but with not as much success. In 1913 the county final between Baltinglass and Newcastle was played in Jones' Road (site of Croke Park today) because that was where the two railway lines met. Wicklow made some mistakes in the early years of the GAA that were to prove costly. For example, Wicklow were to play Clare in Athlone in the first match under GAA rules. Wicklow refused to play because it was too far away. Such a small-minded mentality cost the Garden County a place in the history books.

In-fighting was also the bane of Wicklow GAA. But with the arrival of Micko that mindset has begun to disintegrate. Micko has begun to break the mould that has shaped Wicklow GAA for so long. When he arrived Micko said that he would bring improvements which would be a step in the right direction. Peter feels that Micko needs to stay for another two or three years to continue the work he started in 2006. The last three years have been marvellous and Peter would dearly love to see them continue.

PHYSICAL THERAPIST: NOEL MOLLOY

Noel Molloy has been a member of the medical team for the last three years. Before that he was part of the set-up in Carlow under Luke Dempsey and Liam Hayes. In fact he was part of the Carlow back-room team for ten years. Noel, in his own words, does a lot of the "strapping and wrapping."

Up until last year Eamonn Ó Muircheartaigh was also part of the set-up in Wicklow, but he is not involved this year. Noel does not work-full time as a sports therapist. In fact he works in a factory from 8.30 a.m. to 5.00 p.m. Monday to Friday. He does have a clinic on Monday, Wednesday and Friday nights, and attends the Wicklow training sessions on Tuesdays and Thursdays. He is also involved with the Baltinglass team.

Noel trained as a sports injury therapist over a number of years and is constantly updating his skills. He played senior football with his local club, Rathvilly and was also a regular on the Carlow senior football team. He suffered a serious injury in 1994 in which he sustained two broken legs. It was during this time that he took an interest in how the body healed itself and so began his training in sports injury therapy. His own rehabillitation consisted of cycling, walking and swimming. Three years later he was back playing senior football with Rathvilly under the management of former Dublin player Paul Curran.

By 1999 he had retired from playing, but his interest in training and sports therapy continued to grow. He was asked to become his club team's masseur and became involved with Wicklow when Kevin O'Brien asked him to come on board.

One of Noel's tricks is the use of veterinary tape for strapping joints. Noel's reason is that it is very good at what it is supposed to do - and it doesn't stick to hairs. Noel mixes his own oils. His base oil is grape seed oil and then he mixes other oils with this depending on the needs at the time.

Like all good physiotherapists, Noel emphasises the need to stretch. Stretching is vital to loosen the muscle fibres. Stretching should be progressive and gentle without any sudden movement. The basic stretches for all are the quads, calves, hamstrings and achilles tendons.

As for himself, Noel likes to run when he gets the chance. He has often run with Ireland's international hurdler TJ Kearns. One of Noel's clients is Tony Garland, a transplant athlete.

Noel, like many a team physio, is often regarded as a counsellor. Often, a player will talk to him and tell him things that might be on his mind that he would be reluctant to tell some of the management team. Noel will then be able to make the player's feelings known to the powers-that-be.

A healthy atmosphere is necessary to build up team spirit, and Mick O'Dwyer is one man who can engender team spirit. From the moment of his arrival the interest in Wicklow football took off as never before. Micko has the ability to bring out the best in players. And what's more, he loves the crack and is well able to give as good as he gets, especially from Arthur.

WATERMAN: MARTIN LOTT

The man who is responsible for the water is Martin Lott. Martin is from Barndarrig and played both hurling and football at club level. Martin was not the original waterman. That honour fell to Ray Menton and occasionally Martin would deputise. Last season Martin took on the role full time. The waterman is also responsible for looking after the ice baths. Since being appointed he has attended all training sessions of the senior footballers.

Whereas the kitman Jimmy Whittle sources the water, Martin collects and distributes it. Although Kerry Spring is the official water, River Rock was being used in the early part of the year. So what volume of water is needed by a senior inter county football team? For a training session the waterman brings four dozen 500ml bottles of water, but twice this much to a match. Players are encouraged to drink plenty of water and to bring some home with them as well.

The day of the Tommy Murphy Cup Final in 2008 was Martin's first time to be on the sideline in Croke Park. After thirtty years of going to games in headquarters he finally got to sit on the sideline.

Martin has seen a huge number of players pass through the panel in the time he has beem with the team. In the early rounds of the league there were only about seven or eight of last year's panel in the starting fifteen. In the 1990s Wicklow almost made the breakthrough in Leinster. Unfortunately that did not happen. Quite simply, Wicklow footballers are not used to winning. While there has always been a good core on the team, there panel was always short of two or three to give the edge that was needed to break the mould.

The uncertainty over Thomas Walsh is most frustrating. If Walsh were to return to Carlow, Martin says that he would have no hesitation in shaking his hand and wishing him all the best.

CHEF: EDDIE CASHIN

The man who is a vital ingredient in every evening training session is Eddie Cashin. Eddie grew up in Dunlavin but did not play football. He was a chef in the army for close on thirty years. He was posted in the Curragh for about twenty years and has been stationed in the Glen of Imaal since. I knew that the army had a firing range in the Glen, but I was unaware that there was a permanent army camp there. Eddie tells me that there are about thirty-five people stationed in the Glen.

When I asked him how he had become involved with the team he said that it all happened by accident during Hugh Kenny's time as manager of the county team. Wicklow were due to play a challenge match against Kildare in Ballymore and Hugh asked Eddie if he could prepare some sandwiches for after the game for the two teams. Hugh obviously liked the sandwiches and asked Eddie if he could do the same for training. Eddie did the costing and reported that it would be more economical to provide a meal rather than sandwiches. He has provided the post-training meal ever since and claims to have only missed one session in six years.

And what of the menu? Chicken curry and chicken with rice go down well. Other options are stew or lasagne, shepherd's pie, and steak or chicken dishes. There are always some breads, yoghurt and fruit as well. Drinks include water, tea, milk and fruit juice.

Most of the panel are not fussy about what they eat. Some prefer to make sandwiches after training. Since Wicklow do not have a fixed training base, unlike Kildare for example, it is difficult to give a fixed menu such as roast beef. Micko is not a fussy eater – nor are the rest of the back-room team. The post training meal is usually a time to relax and to have a bit of a laugh. Players finish their meal and drift away. The back-room team are usually the last to leave. On some occasions Micko will drive back to Waterville - at least six hours away. The only occasion that Eddie was not present to serve the post training meal was on the Thursday before the Kildare match in late July. Eddie had booked his holidays many months before not realising that the team would still be involved in the championship this late in the season. Realistically who would have thought that a side rated thirty-first of the thirty-two counties just a couple of years ago would be among the last twelve in the 2009 championship? The final post training meal of the 2009 season was therefore provided in Lawless' Hotel Aughrim.

PHYSIOTHERAPIST: PREMNATH MARGABANDAN (AKA PREM)

Prem first became involved with the team on Easter Sunday for the league match against Carlow. Prem is a chartered physiotherapist and was born in India. He graduated in 1998 and then completed his masters in physiotherapy. He has been in Ireland for two years now.

Before coming to Ireland he lived in Malaysia. His interest is in sports physiotherapy and he joined the Canadian Association of Physiotherapy while in Malaysia. He was physio to the Malaysian Paralympics team in 2004 and 2005 while based in Kuala Lumpar. He came to Ireland in 2007 and is working as a physiotherapist with the HSE in Bray. It was through the team doctor, Brendan Cuddihy that Prem was first approached to become involved in the Wicklow team. He was put in touch with county administrator Michael Murphy and terms were agreed.

SPINEOLOGIST: PAT KELLY

Spineologst Pat Kelly is a member of the Dunlavin Club. He told me that spineology is a therapy that began about thirty years ago. Its origins are in the human potential movement, a movement that strives for humans to reach their maximum genetic potential. While talking to Pat about his therapy I was amazed at the number of overlaps between his practice and those of bio energist Hazel Devine and herbalist Bernadette O'Connor. All three seem to me striving for their clients to reach their maximum potential by channeling their energy levels. Pat has been involved for three years with the Wicklow footballers.

In the changing room I would often see him manipulating the players and they would groan in agony, but would seem to benefit from their pain. Occasionally I would jeer the players on the couch that it was not doing them any good unless it was hurting them. Pat explained to me that he manipulates the vertebrae by reading the surrounding muscles. He gives a little shock to the muscle which brings the vertebrae back into alignment. Occasionally the client will hear a crack. This, Pat tells me, is simply gas that is trapped between the vertebrae being released. He also tells me that it is proven that there is a reduction in pulled muscles when the vertebrae are correctly aligned. Paul Earls who used to suffer regularly from pulled hamstrings agrees with this – since he began receiving treatment from Pat he has not had as many problems with his hamstring.

Pat told me that Peter Keogh was the only member of the team/panel/backroom team who had not received treatment. Peter still refused but remarked that soon I would be fighting for my place on the team. The following Thursday Pat invited me onto the table and performed his magic. It is a regret of mine that I did not start receiving treatment from him months ago – and it only takes a few minutes.

Index